MW01115590

TAKING DISCIPLESHIP SERIOUSLY

A RADICAL BIBLICAL APPROACH

TOM SINE

Judson Press ® Valley Forge

TAKING DISCIPLESHIP SERIOUSLY

Copyright © 1985
Judson Press, Valley Forge, PA 19482-0851

Library of Congress Cataloging in Publication Data
Sine, Tom.
   Taking discipleship seriously.
   Includes bibliographical references.
   1. Christian life—1960-   2. Evangelistic work.
I. Title.
BV4501.2.S4725   1985   248.4   85-7601
ISBN 0-8170-1085-8

Printed in the U.S.A.
05 04 03 02 01 00 99 98 97
9 8 7 6

Foreword

For an evangelical such as I, the clear call to a *radical, biblical* discipleship is unique. It was little heard in evangelical Christianity in years gone by. In this book Tom Sine does a service for the whole church, but especially for the evangelical wing of the church.

The thrust is threefold. Christian faith is not private. Rightful concern for personal salvation cannot stop with personal morality. A disciple *is* one who, when converted, embarks upon a lifelong search for a clear, strong, even passionate, relationship with God. A disciple *is* a learner, studying God's record of revelation to know God more clearly and to understand God's purpose most surely. A disciple *is* one who seeks to win others to faith in God through Jesus Christ. A disciple recognizes that God is concerned with planet Earth. Issues of world peace and justice are God's issues.

Second, Sine's book is *radical*. He dares to read Jesus carefully and comes out as Bonhoeffer did, with costly grace. (This tells us something about evangelism—the need for "truth in advertising." The same Jesus who promises peace and joy through reconciliation with God calls us to take up the cross!) This book will make you uneasy. It demands that discipleship reach into our very economic lifestyles.

Finally, Sine constantly lifts up the *urgency* of moving into radical, biblical discipleship. For him, there is not a lot of time. The call to share the gospel, ourselves, and our means is passionately urgent.

Emmett Johnson

With appreciation to Doug Coe, who took time to disciple a young man; to E. Stanley Jones, who helped me to understand that discipleship is integrally related to mission; and to Chavannes Jeune, who has taught me with his life what it means to be a disciple of Jesus Christ.

Contents

Introduction

Increasing numbers of Christians are asking questions about discipleship, partly out of interest and partly out of confusion! We are interested because many of us are taking our faith more seriously than ever before and want the practice of that faith to make a difference to the world. But we are also confused because there are so many different notions of what discipleship means.

For some, discipleship is simply a matter of being an active member in the local church. For others, discipleship is seen as the growth of private spiritual life through Bible study and prayer. Still others see discipleship as a public commitment to work for justice and peace.

Almost all Christians seem to narrow discipleship to one compartment in their already busy lives. I am not sure that we, as contemporary Christians, have understood the radical nature of Christ's call.

This book will attempt to cut through this confusion and present a radically biblical approach to discipleship that has implications for every area of our lives and for the larger mission of the church.

Jesus began his ministry nearly two millenia ago, inviting people to follow him. A few did. He is still inviting. There are still a few who are willing to follow.

Listen to what he expects of his followers: "Anyone who wishes to be a follower of mine must leave self behind; he [or she] must take up his [or her] cross, and come with me. Whoever cares for his [or her] own safety is lost; but if a man [or woman] will . . . be lost for my sake and for the Gospel, that man [or woman] is safe. What does a man [or woman] gain by winning the whole world at the cost of his [or her] true self?" (Mark 8:34-36, NEB).

And at another time Jesus discussed the cost of discipleship with his followers:

> As they were going along the road a man said to him, "I will follow you wherever you go." Jesus answered, "Foxes have their holes, the birds their roosts; but the Son of Man has nowhere to lay his head." To another he said, "Follow me," but the man replied, "Let me go and bury my father first." Jesus said, "Leave the dead to bury their dead; you must go and announce the kingdom of God."
> Yet another said, "I will follow you, sir; but let me first say good-bye to my people at home." To him Jesus said, "No one who sets his hand to plough and then keeps looking back is fit for the king-dom of God" (Luke 9:57-62, NEB).

As we listen to the radical demands of Christ's call, we often find ourselves in the words of John Alexander going "to great lengths claiming He didn't teach what He clearly did. We have to, of course. To admit He taught what He did would require us either to change (repent) or to criticize Him. And neither of those is acceptable. So we obfuscate. The problem is that Jesus was an extremist, and we are moderates. His evaluation of our way of life was that it is upside down."[1]

If we take Jesus seriously, it will mean literally turning our lives upside down. Following him will not only mean getting our spiritual lives together or only being active at church, it will also mean putting aside all of our lesser agenda and seeking first the kingdom. It will mean that Jesus will begin to transform every area of our lives, our values, priorities, attitudes, and even our lifestyles. This commitment will also mean joining communities of shared life and mission trying to make a difference in the world.

If we are going to take discipleship seriously, we must take the Master seriously and not try to explain away his radical call. If we are to be his disciples, we need to set aside our conventional and comfortable notions of discipleship and follow Jesus—without looking back.

[1]Donald B. Kraybill, *The Upside-Down Kingdom* (Scottdale, Pennsylvania: Herald Press, 1978), p. 13.

Goals of This Book

If we are to follow Christ, we must understand as fully as possible what it means to be a disciple. The goals of this book are to enable the reader:

1. To understand something of the history and meaning of discipleship in our Judeo-Christian heritage.
2. To become more aware of some of the urgent problems facing our world today and tomorrow.
3. To understand more fully God's intentions for that world.
4. To discover what it means to be a disciple as a member of the body of Jesus Christ in the world.
5. To learn how we can grow as disciples, more fully incarnate the values, and seek first the intentions of God's kingdom in life and mission.
6. To become aware of a broad spectrum of creative ways in which disciples are investing their lives and resources to further the kingdom in the world.
7. To learn how to enable others in the body of Christ to become more serious and faithful disciples of Jesus Christ.

This discussion is going to take place in the context of a rapidly changing global and national future as well as in the context of a dramatically changing denominational future for main-line Protestant churches.

Looking to the Fields

Before we focus on the purposes of God or on the meaning of discipleship, we need to look to the horizon. Jesus challenges us to "look to fields that are white unto harvest."

In a time of rapid change we need to look to fields both as they are today and as they will be tomorrow. We need to anticipate the global, national, and denominational changes that are likely to confront us as we approach the twenty-first century. Even as Jesus trained his disciples to serve in an as yet uncharted future, so we look to the future in which we are called to live as disciples.

Global Futures

Since we are involved in programs of international mission, it is important that we understand something of how global context is changing; that is, if we are to be disciples of Jesus Christ, we must be world Christians. Emerging challenges represent emerging opportunities for disciples of Jesus Christ to respond in creative new ways. Let's look now at how the global context of our discipleship is changing.

As we near the year 2000 we will be sharing this planet with some 6.2 billion people. Of course, much of that growth is going

to take place in the developing nations. Forecasts indicate that in regions like the Indian subcontinent, Africa, and parts of Asia, food production won't keep pace with population growth.

Today, approximately 800 million of our neighbors live in what is called absolute poverty—below basic subsistence. Those people make less than ninety dollars per person per year and their children suffer from chronic malnutrition. Tragically, millions of others face starvation.

So the forecast isn't bright. As the end of the century approaches, the numbers of hungry people are likely to increase incredibly. (That is why I asserted in *The Mustard Seed Conspiracy*, "The party is over!")

The great consumer party with "ever more" lifestyles that we have enjoyed in the West since the end of World War II is now over, especially for the world's poor. Many won't even survive unless we find a more just way to use the planet's resources and productive power. Those of us who are Christians need a more biblical and responsible view of stewardship.

Many people, not realizing the party is over, still press into the cities to try to get a "piece of the action." Consequently, we face an unprecedented urban population explosion in our lifetimes. Mexico City will be the largest city in the world by the year 2000, with 32 million people. São Paulo will be the second largest, with 25 million. Calcutta and Bombay will have 19 million each. *Time* magazine has described this growth as an urban apocalypse because these urban corridors are completely unable to sustain or support such a level of growth.

Global environmental, economic, and political trends are also notable. Millions of acres of arable land are being lost to deserts and environmental degradation. Increasingly, the planet is becoming a large garbage dump in which rich and poor alike live in the midst of their waste.

In addition, America's enormous deficit places pressure on the global economic system. And poorer nations are now in debt $900 billion to wealthier nations. If those nations default, major economic disruption will ensue among all nations.

Growing political destabilization will continue to swell the ranks of the nearly nine million refugees in the world today. This growing refugee population also represents a growing opportunity for the church to respond in compassion.

The church can also respond to the threat of nuclear war which hangs over the entire world. For until the Soviets and the United States negotiate a reduction in nuclear arms that is mutual and verifiable, the two superpowers will not have the moral clout necessary to influence smaller nations to sign a nuclear nonproliferation treaty. Failing to get the smaller nations to sign a nuclear nonproliferation treaty will result in thirty to forty nations gaining access to nuclear weapons by the year 2000, and the odds are that those weapons would be used within ten years. Disciples are also called to work for peace, particularly in a world like ours.

I have a growing concern that the United States might attempt military intervention in Central America. I am also fearful for the sanctuary churches (churches that shelter refugees from deportation) in the United States.

Ralph Winter at the Center for World Mission will tell us that we are going backwards in world evangelization. Population growth is outstripping our ability to share Christ with a number of unreached groups. We spend about 5 percent of our evangelism dollars to reach those who have never heard the gospel of Jesus Christ. We need many more disciples trained and called into cross-cultural evangelism.

Recently I have worked with two American evangelical denominations that have become "Third World" denominations in the last two years. The Covenant Church and the Church of God (out of Anderson, Indiana) now have more members in developing countries than they have in the United States.

What this means is that the leadership of the church is shifting. The days of paternalism are over. By the year 2000 over half of all Christians in the world will be in the Southern Hemisphere. They will be poorer, younger, politically more radical, and probably more than a little upset with the way their rich neighbors are using up the planet's resources. As those neighbors, we need to learn to work in true partnership and to share leadership. As disciples, we will need to learn to read African, Asian, and Latin American theology. Clearly, tomorrow's world will be increasingly transnational.

National Futures

As disciples of Jesus Christ in the United States, it is important that we also understand how our national context is changing. Our country has undergone major demographic change. The traditional nuclear family where "only Dad works" now represents only about 17 percent of the population. In the last ten years we have seen a dramatic increase in the number of singles and single-parent families, yet our churches still target their ministry almost exclusively to the nuclear family.

American culture is becoming much more racially pluralistic. If you are white and live in California, in the year 2000 you will be in the minority. By that date the population of California will be at least one-half Hispanic. Hispanics are the most rapidly growing ethnic population in the United States. Black population is also growing, while white population growth in America is relatively static. This means that not only will we have a much more ethnically pluralistic society in the future, but also we will be provided with an opportunity for the church to become more pluralistic.

I forecast in *The Mustard Seed Conspiracy*, which was completed about the time of the 1981 presidential inauguration, that there would be a widening gap between the rich and the poor in the United States. In fact, I said that "while the seventies were the 'Decade of Me; the eighties are likely to be the 'Decade of Us and Them.'"[2]

I am even more convinced, as of the 1985 inauguration, that we are likely to see growing polarization between the haves and the have-nots in our society. The cutbacks necessary to bring our $200 billion deficit in line will not come primarily from defense cuts. We can expect social programs to be slashed even further. It's a question of how much suffering will take place before the churches respond or the poor react in anger.

Seniors and the young are likely to be among those who suffer most. Seniors on fixed incomes represent the "new poor" of the eighties. Increasingly they are having to choose between buying food or fuel. They often can't afford both.

We are creating a permanent underclass of young people who will live and die in America and never have jobs. It's not because they are lazy or shiftless; they simply haven't received enough education in their urban schools to fill out an application form! They

[2]Tom Sine, *The Mustard Seed Conspiracy* (Waco, Texas: Word Books, 1981), p. 51.

have no job skills and would have no jobs in their communities even if they did have literacy skills. The upturn in the economy simply won't influence this kind of structural unemployment.

But there are some disciples of Jesus Christ who have found a way to have an influence. Tom Skinner and Associates have rented a building across the street from an inner-city high school in Newark, New Jersey. In that building they have set up a complete computer training program which includes basic literacy skills. High school youth are desperately trying to get into the program; they know if they successfully complete the training, they will never be unemployed again.

This and other programs can help youth whose families cannot be supportive. For while the breakup of families in many parts of the country seems to be leveling off, violence within families seems to be on the increase. Abuse toward women and children in certain communities is reaching almost epidemic proportions. Surely the church could become a more effective force for reconciliation in these families.

There are other issues to which the church also must respond. Abortion was for many Christians the only ethical issue in the 1984 election. What hasn't been clear to many Christians is that we are facing a literal explosion of a new ethical issues in bio-ethics, genetics, and bionics.

For example, in a story about sperm banks in which a woman selected from a catalog sperm with which she chose to be impregnated, the subtitle of the article was "You don't have to meet Mr. Right—all you have to do is buy his genes." Those who follow Christ must get in touch with the issues of our times and struggle to find a biblical perspective.

Computers and robotics and the decentralization of television technology will dramatically change our society in the next ten years. These systems will provide new capabilities in our personal lives, professions, and churches. They will also raise a spectrum of new ethical issues from invasion of privacy to elimination of entry-level jobs.

Against this backdrop of a world in flux, I also want to report that a growing edge of the church is in renewal. For example, a church in Plain City, Ohio, sent seven of its members to Haiti for a two-year involvement in construction, agriculture, and handicrafts. They are expressing their discipleship in enabling their Haitian brothers and sisters to become more self-reliant.

University Baptist Church in Seattle has voted overwhelmingly to use its church building as a sanctuary for undocumented refugees from El Salvador. This action has brought about a remarkable revitalization of congregational life as members put themselves on the line for their growing family of those who have escaped torture, persecution, and death in El Salvador.

There is a renewing edge in the church of Jesus Christ. Churches can respond to the changing world in ways which affect its course. And many have. Many more are called to respond. All of these emerging challenges are in fact emerging opportunities for those of us who comprise the fellowship of disciples of Jesus.

Denominational Futures

Beyond looking at the global and national future, it is imperative to gain some sense of how main-line Protestant churches are changing if we are to be effective disciples. Not only are national demographics changing, so are denominational demographics. I will refer to American Baptist Churches in the U.S.A. as an example.

Even as American society is becoming more ethnically pluralistic, so are American Baptist churches. Both the black and Hispanic populations in the denomination are growing while the white growth is static. While the denomination is becoming more pluralistic, membership growth is almost nil. New churches open in the Southwest while older ones close in the Northeast. American Baptists have recently embarked on a "Grow By Caring" program, hoping once again to get the denomination "on the grow."

American Baptists are also an aging denomination. The projected median age for white members in 1990 will be sixty years and for nonwhites, fifty years. That explains in part why church school attendance and baptisms have fallen almost 50 percent since 1950.

One has to wonder, if membership growth doesn't increase and the denomination continues to age, what will happen to its financial base? Given the demographic trends, finances are likely to decline. In view of the global and national challenges facing us in the eighties and nineties, we will need significantly *more* resources directed into Christian mission, not less. As those who want to follow Christ seriously in discipleship, we need to explore how to direct more of our institutional and personal resources into mission. This will probably become a major denominational issue since American Baptists have a very high commitment to global and domestic mission.

The fields certainly are ripe unto harvest. The world today and tomorrow is exploding with opportunities. The emerging challenges of the eighties and nineties are indeed emerging opportunities for the people of God to act with compassion, imagination, and faith.

As we begin this journey together to learn what it means to be biblical disciples, I think it is clear that it means more than focusing on our own private Christian growth. It means more than keeping the institutional church operating. To be a disciple of Jesus Christ means that we must look outward as he did. As he was a man for others, we need to become people for others. Even as his compassion embraced a world, we pray that he will give us eyes to see beyond our own personal situations to the world in which he calls his disciples to serve.

This book is intentionally designed to be used as a study book in discipleship for adult church school classes, small group discussions, and college classes. Questions are included at the end of each chapter to help focus discussion and challenge participants to move toward application.

1
CHAPTER

Discipleship and the Master

"Christianity without discipleship is always Christianity without Christ,"[1] declared Dietrich Bonhoeffer. He is absolutely right. The Christ who calls us from the pages of the New Testament always calls us to follow him. Unless we acknowledge his lordship over us and follow him in every aspect of life, we are left with a "Christianity without Christ." We are left with yet another religion in which we are the masters because we have refused to follow the Master.

If we are to follow, we must understand who this One is that calls us and understand what he expects from us. This chapter will seek to help us:

1. Understand the historical uniqueness of Christ's call to discipleship;
2. More fully grasp who this One is who calls us;
3. More clearly hear his call and understand his expectations for our lives.

Historical Uniqueness of Christ's Call

Discipleship was not unique to the first followers of Jesus. For centuries the Jews had programs to disciple the faithful. "And they

[1] Dietrich Bonhoeffer, *The Cost of Discipleship* (New York: Macmillan Publishing Company, Inc., 1957), p. 52.

cast lots for their duties, all alike, the small as well as the great, the teacher *as well* as the pupil" (1 Chronicles 25:8). The teachers of ancient Israel tutored their pupils in an understanding and interpretation of the Torah as the basis of faith and life.

God's intention from the beginning was to create a people different from others around them. If they faithfully followed their Creator's tutelage, they would not only be reconciled to God but also become a culturally transformed people . . . in their worship, values, culture, relationships, health principles, and just economic practices.

In "Fiddler on the Roof" we see Tevye desperately struggling to reconcile the changing times with the changeless principles of his faith. In exasperation he exclaims, "I cannot bend anymore or I will break!" and launches into that marvelous ballad: "Tradition, tradition. . . !"

As the Jews have struggled to maintain their tradition, their uniqueness, and their calling in a broad spectrum of alien cultures, the Torah has been their touchstone to God. Jewish teachers have over the centuries sought to enable disciples to understand and interpret the implications of the Torah in every dimension of life and culture.

In 2 Kings 2:3 we note the beginning of the schools of the prophets. The Jews institutionalized a number of formal schooling programs not only to educate disciples, but also to educate those who could lead the community to live out faithfully the radical countercultural demands of their faith.

It was out of this heritage that, four hundred years later, a man appeared in the wilderness of Judea. He came proclaiming, "Make ready the way of the Lord, make His paths straight" (Mark 1:3). John the Baptist came challenging people to repent and confess their sins. He came prophesying the emergence of a new order, declaring "the axe is already laid at the root. . . . His winnowing fork is in His hand, and He will burn up the chaff with unquenchable fire" (Matthew 3: 10, 12).

Once again God had spoken and called this people to follow in repentance and faithfulness. People were baptized, the established order was upset, and there was a stirring in the land.

"In the fullness of time" Christ came. He came preaching the message that the kingdom of God had arrived. He came healing the sick, giving sight to the blind, and lifting the downcast. And he came inviting people to follow him.

As Jesus Christ invited those first disciples, Peter and Andrew, to follow him, he totally upset the traditional Jewish notion of what it meant to be a disciple (Mark 3:13-15). As Orlando Costas points out,

"The rabbinic disciples chose their teachers . . ."[2] while Christ invited those that he chose to follow him. The master, not the pupils, initiated this new relationship of discipling.

The rabbis instructed their disciples to follow the Torah. Jesus, in a radical departure from orthodoxy, instructed his disciples to follow him. His life and teachings became the new curriculum, the new wine, the new interpretation of traditional faith.

The rabbis declared that their authority came from Moses, that they were "the disciples of Moses." They asked, in effect, of Jesus, "Who in the world are you? From where does your authority come?" They were really asking Jesus and his disciples how they could possibly have any authority to teach when they had not been taught in properly recognized schools. Jesus and his disciples were, after all, obviously "ignorant and unlearned men." Yet, even though he hadn't been to the proper schools, people recognized Jesus as having remarkable authority. "And amazement came upon them all, and they *began* discussing with one another, and saying, 'What is this message? For with authority and power He commands the unclean spirits, and they come out'" (Luke 4:36).

Entering rabbinic schools involved commitment to an educational task. Entering the school of Christ is an open-ended commitment both to discipleship and to devotion to Christ.

And, finally, instead of running a formal, institutional educational program, Christ chose a different methodology. He formed a community of brothers and sisters who shared common life together and learned together. In the context of this organic community he operated his informal school of discipleship. He used everything as grist for curriculum—from personal failure and relational conflict to small children and the rural beauty of Judea and Samaria.

Instead of focusing his attention on the masses, Jesus focused his attention on those he had chosen. He spent hours pouring his life into his followers, particularly into the twelve. He explained the parables, taught his disciples from their mistakes, and washed their feet.

One thing in Christ's approach to discipleship, however, was not much different from the traditional approach: the call to be countercultural. In fact, if anything, his call to his disciples to be radically counter to the prevailing culture was dramatically pronounced. Jesus called his followers then as now not only to commit themselves to God and follow the way but also to transform radically their fundamental values and life priorities and commit themselves to be full-time agents of the kingdom.

[2]Orlando E. Costas, *The Integrity of Mission: The Inner Life and Outreach of the Church* (New York: Harper & Row, Publishers, Inc., 1979), p. 15.

So Jesus comes inviting, calling, and teaching those who would follow. Who is this One who so compellingly calls us to follow and what does it mean to be his disciple today?

The Master and the Call

Who indeed is this One who still calls us across the centuries to follow? Undeniably he is a teacher. He seems to come to us as a breath of fresh air in every time and culture. His stories intrigue us, his paradoxes bewilder us, and this kingdom he talks about tugs at a hope very deep within us.

We watch in stark disbelief as he gives sight to the blind, makes the palsied whole, cleanses lepers, and even raises the dead. Slowly we become aware that this One is more than a teacher, more than a moral example. He comes to us not only with authority but also with a special grace that reaches out to us in the midst of all the struggles of our lives.

Suddenly we realize that this Jesus does not summon us to follow him simply as a teacher or moral example but as Christ the Son of the living God. Jesus declares that "he that has seen me has seen the Father." In the servant life, the criminal death, and the triumphant resurrection of Jesus Christ, God is fully disclosed to us. Jesus asked his disciples who they thought he was. "Simon Peter answered and said, 'Thou art the Christ, the Son of the living God.' And Jesus answered and said to him, 'Blessed are you, Simon Barjona, because flesh and blood did not reveal *this* to you, but My Father who is in heaven'" (Matthew 16:16-17). Peter declared the divinity of Jesus Christ publicly after his resurrection, "Let all the house of Israel therefore know assuredly that God has made him both Lord and Christ, this Jesus whom you crucified" (Acts 2:38, RSV). And Paul declared that at the end of history, "every knee should bow . . . and every tongue confess that Jesus Christ is Lord, to the glory of God . . ." (Philippians 2:10-11, RSV).

> The divine claim to all things created in heaven and on earth is very concretely Jesus' claim. Behind that claim lies not only the deity of Christ, but also the work of his death and resurrection. For in that act, he has reestablished the divine authority over the fallen order and introduced a new Kingdom that unifies under one banner the powers of heaven and the glories of earth. Now it can be said that there is no purpose or promise of creation that is not fulfilled in principle in the reign of Jesus Christ.[3]

The resurrected Christ is not only Master, Lord, and King but

---

[3] William A. Dyrness, *Let The Earth Rejoice!: A Biblical Theology of Holistic Mission* (Westchester, Illinois: Crossway Books, 1983), p. 147.

the purpose of God reaching incarnationally into human history. Jesus Christ is . . . a reach into history of that aspect of the godhead that has been already in lively and agonizing engagement with the world. Gabriel Fackre goes on to affirm, "The risen Christ is the conqueror who opened the future and assures the coming kingdom."[4]

Here then is the Christ who stands at the threshold of history and invites us to follow. Now that we have some glimpse of who he is, it is even more essential that we understand what it means to follow him.

Expectations for Discipleship

Tony Campolo said he was raised to believe that being saved was a matter of believing "all the right things and saying yes to the right questions. . . ."[5] For some, this business of following Christ is simply a matter of being an active church person and keeping the wheels of the local church turning. While that's important, it isn't necessarily all that discipleship is about.

For others, being a Christian is simply a matter of "commitment by association." If one hangs around a church building, it is automatically assumed that one is Christian. One can no more assume to be following Jesus than one can assume that one is married. There must be a clear declaration and commitment.

[4]Gabriel Fackre, *The Christian Story* (Grand Rapids, Michigan: William B. Eerdmans Publishing Co., 1978), p. 96.

[5]Anthony Campolo, *A Reasonable Faith: Responding to Secularism* (Waco, Texas: Word, Inc., 1983), p. 170.

For still others, being a Christian means joining the local church and making a profession of faith. While this action provides a clear point of entry into the institutional church, it is not always based on a personal commitment to follow Jesus Christ in discipleship.

If believing the right things, giving the right answers, joining and actively participating in the local church aren't necessarily discipleship, what is?

Let's go back to the Bible and see what it meant to be a disciple of Jesus in the beginning, before there was a church. Let's go to Galilee and follow the Master as he walks the dusty roads of this small Roman colony.

> And walking by the Sea of Galilee, He saw two brothers, Simon who was called Peter, and Andrew his brother, casting a net into the sea; for they were fishermen. And He said to them, "Follow Me, and I will make you fishers of men." And they immediately left the nets, and followed Him. And going on from there He saw two other brothers, James the *son* of Zebedee, and John his brother, in the boat with Zebedee their father, mending their nets; and He called them. And they immediately left the boat and their father, and followed Him. And *Jesus* was going about in all Galilee, teaching in their synagogues, and proclaiming the gospel of the kingdom, and healing every kind of disease and every kind of sickness among the people (Matthew 4:18-23).

First, it is important to note that Jesus must have used different criteria for selecting those who would join him in ministry than we tend to use in the church today. He didn't call the prominent, affluent community leaders or seminary graduates. He called a collection of terribly ordinary people, many from the unpleasant fringes of Jewish society, some of whom we probably wouldn't want in our churches. He called not only fishermen but tax collectors and political revolutionaries. Unlike the rabbinical schools, Jesus included women among his disciples as well. He also spent a surprising amount of time with children.

In other words, Jesus called an extremely ordinary group of people to follow him who apparently had no special education or prestige to lend to the movement. It was to this group that he would ultimately entrust the future of the faith.

Jesus is still calling ordinary people to follow, regardless of education, abilities, or background. He is not interested in those things that may set us apart; he is interested in us for ourselves.

When Jesus calls us to follow, he is not looking for occasional use of our gifts on the weekends. He wants our lives. Peter and Andrew understood that. So did James and John and dozens of other men and women that we never meet in the pages of the Scriptures. Jesus expects us to give him everything. "If anyone comes to Me, and does not hate his own father and mother and wife and children and brothers and sisters, yes, and even his own life, he cannot be My disciple. Whoever does not carry his own cross and come after Me cannot be My disciple" (Luke 14:26-27).

In other words, even though Jesus called very ordinary people, his was a very extraordinary call. It wasn't a matter of working in some meetings over the weekend or volunteering a little time to help with a crusade. Jesus expected those whom he called to drop their nets, quit their jobs, leave their families, and follow him. He expected them to carry a cross and, if so called, to be crucified on it. That is discipleship.

In contemporary churches in which we expect little from our people and are satisfied with even less, it is really hard for us to take Jesus' call to the cross seriously. "Christians spend a lot of time and energy explaining why Jesus couldn't possibly have meant what he said. This is understandable: Jesus is an extremist, and we are all moderates. What is worse, he was an extremist in his whole life—not just some narrowly 'spiritual' areas . . . but in everything,"[6] observes John Alexander. Jesus expects those who follow him to be as extreme as his first followers were in putting aside every lesser thing and making this business of being a disciple a whole-life proposition.

For some it may indeed mean leaving jobs to join Christ's itinerant mission band. For others it may mean leaving loved ones to devote one's life to the work of the kingdom in Mexico City or Calcutta.

For all of us it will mean taking Jesus seriously and putting him and his agenda at the very center of our lives. We need to remember that his agenda for the kingdom hasn't changed since he called those first disciples. We are still challenged to heal the sick, proclaim good news to the captive, and restore sight to the blind. As disciples we are all called to be involved actively and regularly in making a difference for the kingdom in our own society—right now.

How can ordinary people respond to this extraordinary call? Where do we begin? We begin as Peter and Andrew did. We begin by turning our back on all that has captured our time, energy, and resources. We begin by turning and following Jesus. We begin by sitting at his feet and learning from him. We begin by recognizing that God *is* and that God reaches out in love through Jesus Christ to bring us back to our Creator. Once we decide to turn to God we must, like the prodigal, also turn away from the past. We must, in repentance, turn away from all that was destroying us, our lives, and relationships, and through the One who died in our stead find new beginnings and forgiveness of our sins.

[6]John Alexander, "Why We Must Ignore Jesus," *The Other Side*, October 1977, p. 8.

Jesus Christ calls all of us, whether we are church members or not, to repent of our sins and of the tyranny of self and to surrender our lives to the recreating power of God. Through faith in Christ and faith in Christ alone we will be changed. God desires nothing less than to enable broken, selfish persons like us to begin maturing into kingdom persons who begin learning how to live for God and others. Paul has assured us that "God, who began this good work in you, will carry it on until it is finished on the Day of Christ Jesus" (Philippians 1:6, TEV).

If you have never made the decision to become a serious follower of Jesus Christ, there's no reason you can't do so now. All it requires is turning to Christ in prayer, confession, and commitment. Find those in your congregation who are serious about their faith to help you to start growing in your discipleship.

E. Stanley Jones affirms that "self surrender is the greatest emancipation that ever comes to a human being. Seek first the kingdom of God and all things will be added to you including yourself."[7] Jesus wasn't kidding. It really is in losing life that we find life. God has made every cell of our being for the kingdom.

> As we surrender our lives to loving our Father and others he begins changing us into the integrated, delightful kingdom people he intended us to be. However, the surrender of ourselves to the life-transforming lordship of Christ cannot be limited to the private, personal, pietistic compartment of our lives. Jesus in his extremism insists that we surrender all our relationships, our resources, our careers, our futures—our total lives—to his lordship.
>
> Not surprisingly, a number of people during his life and ministry and since that time have felt the price is too high. But those few who gladly relinquish all they have to possess the pearl of great price not only experience the personal redemption of God; they become collaborators with him in the redemption of a world.[8]

"To be Christian is to be possessed and dominated by the kingdom of God," Jim Wallis explains. "Salvation must not be seen as merely an individual event in which the individual has a part. The kingdom of God has come to transform the world and us with it by the power of God in Jesus Christ. The cross of Christ is not just the symbol of our atonement but the very pattern and definition of our lives, the very means of the new order that has invaded the world in Christ."[9]

---

[7] E. Stanley Jones, *The Unshakable Kingdom and the Unchanging Person* (Nashville, Tennessee: Abingdon Press, 1972), p. 102.

[8] Tom Sine, *The Mustard Seed Conspiracy: You Can Make a Difference in Tomorrow's Troubled World* (Waco, Texas: Word, Inc., 1981), p. 113.

[9] Jim Wallis, *Agenda for a Biblical People* (New York: Harper & Row, Publishers, Inc., 1978), p. 30.

If the kingdom of God has indeed come not only to transform us but the world, then clearly we are a part of something much larger than just our own personal salvation. The Christ that we follow spoke incessantly of the kingdom. He told us that the "kingdom of God was at hand," "the kingdom of God was very near us." And he also told us, ". . . do not be afraid . . . for your Father has chosen gladly to give you the kingdom" (Luke 12:32).

There is a promise for the empowerment of our discipleship. The Holy Spirit "will convict the world concerning sin, and righteousness, and judgment . . . the Spirit of truth . . . will guide you into all the truth" (John 16:8, 13).

So we are empowered by the Holy Spirit and by these words of Jesus: "In the world you have tribulation, but take courage; I have overcome the world" (16:33).

Jesus taught us to pray a very unusual prayer ". . . thy kingdom come, thy will be done on earth as it is in heaven."

What is this kingdom that Jesus wants us to pray will come on earth? What did he mean when he told those first disciples "to seek first the kingdom"? What does our discipleship have to do with the kingdom of God?

Questions for Discussion

1. How is the discipleship Jesus calls us to different from the Jewish approach to discipleship?

2. What does it mean to be a disciple of Jesus Christ?

3. Outline specific ways in which your discipleship is changing your personal life, your ethics, your family life, your career, your stewardship, and your ministry.

2
CHAPTER

God's Intentions for the
Human Future

"Where *there is* no vision, the people perish," the Scriptures remind us (Proverbs 29:18, KJV). If we are to be disciples of Jesus we must commit ourselves not only to him, but also to his vision for the future. Only as we begin to understand something of his dreams for his people and his world do we have any possibility of working with him to see those dreams realized. This chapter explores what God's intentions are for the human future and how he expects us as disciples of Christ to manifest those intentions in our lives, churches, and world.

Where there is no vision, the people do perish. As disciples of Jesus Christ we need a vision for the future to which we can commit ourselves that is biblical, not cultural.

Examining Some Non-biblical Images for the Future

There is no shortage of secular visions for the future to which people commit their lives. Some espouse a new age of affluence and peace achieved through the transcendence of the human spirit. Marxists look forward to a politically and economically reordered society. Capitalists look forward to a future of ever-increasing economic growth and ever more consumptive lifestyles. Someone has written, "Marxism says all there is is matter and capitalism says all that matters is matter, but they are both materialistic."

As Christians we need a vision for the future that is more than

materialistic and economic. We need a vision that embraces the to-
tality of human experience, a vision that is dependent on the initiative of God, not on human initiative.

Some believers buy into a Christian gradualism in which they
believe the society will slowly improve through the influence of
state, church, and voluntary organizations. People who hold this
viewpoint romantically believe society will inevitably get better. Some
even believe a particular culture could evolve into utopia on earth.

Unfortunately, too many other Christians, in their attempts to find
a biblical approach to the future, get caught up in a nonbiblical
fatalism. For example, while I was making a presentation on world
hunger at a Christian college, a student began waving her hand. I
kept talking. She kept waving her hand. I finally stopped and said,
"What is it?" She responded, "Do you have any idea of what you
said?" I replied, "I don't know, tell me." She said, "You said we
should feed hungry people . . . if we feed hungry people, then
things won't get worse and if things don't get worse, then Jesus
won't come." The logic of that viewpoint would lead us to torpedo
the grain boats going to Africa while saying "Even so, come quickly,
Lord Jesus!"

I have subsequently discovered that the student's question doesn't
represent an isolated point of view. Many Christians have bought
into a deterministic view of history and a fatalistic view of the future
in which they sincerely believe that everything inevitably has to get
worse. Their only hope for the future is that they will escape this
condemned planet to a nonmaterial heaven "out there." The powers
of darkness have conspired through our own end-times eschatology
to convince us that we can't make a difference. Too many of us are
convinced that the church in America, made up of the most affluent,
best educated Christians in the history of the world, can't really be
an influence for the kingdom. That viewpoint is patently absurd.
The Bible calls every generation to be salt, light, and leaven as the
ministering disciples of Jesus Christ.

However, both the Christians who subscribe to a social gradualism and those who are caught in a hopeless fatalism seem to buy
fully into yet another image of the future. We all seem to buy into
the "American Dream" and the philosophy of "looking out for number one." We all seem to devote a major part of our energy, resources, and time into getting our piece of the "Great American Pie"
while the getting is still good.

For those who have been excluded from the mainstream of society
due to racism, poverty, or discrimination, this quest is understandable. It is often an attempt for the excluded to achieve human dignity, but for the rest of us, the dream is often just a quest for lifestyles
of ever more affluence, consumption, and power in a world of growing inequity and deprivation.

Ironically, some Christians are able to believe at one and the same time in two very different views of the future: the first in which they pessimistically believe everything is inevitably going to get worse and worse and the destruction of the planet earth is at hand; and the second in which they optimistically believe the American economy is going to grow 4 percent every year and they are going to enjoy ever more consumptive lifestyles. To illustrate the extent of this dualism, someone has reported that an author of prophetic books that predict the world is going to end tomorrow has invested the profits from those books in long-term American growth bonds!

As followers of Jesus Christ we are called not to seek life; we are called to lose life. We are called not to look out for "number one"; we are called to be that kernel of wheat that falls into the ground and dies. We are called not to be ministered to, but to minister. We are called not to pursue a materialistic future of ever more consumptive living. Even as Jesus was a person for others, we are called to be a people for others. We are called to follow the Master in the pursuit of a very different vision.

A Biblical Vision of the Future of God

If we are to follow Jesus, we must also understand and follow what Elizabeth O'Connor calls her very "disturbing dream."[1] If we are to understand this dream, we must understand its ancient Jewish origins. We must go back to the Old Testament and discern something of the Creator's intentions for the creatures and the created order. What are God's intentions for the human future? Clearly in the creation God's intentions were good. Even after the fall we are told that in Abraham all nations of the world would be blessed.

From the beginning God's intentions were to create a people for God's own self. God selected a people who were no people . . . a very unlikely band of Semitic slaves. God promised them a new future and liberated them from oppression and slavery.

The history of the children of Israel is a turbulent history of their faithful following of the leadership of Yahweh and at other times of their flagrant rebellion against the One who had chosen them, but even in judgment and captivity God never abandoned these children or the commitment to give them a new future. The Jewish people are a people of remembrance and anticipation. They live in remembrance of the acts of God in their past and in anticipation of the promise of God in their future.

What was that promise they expectantly waited for? Listen to the prophet Isaiah.

<hr>

[1] Elizabeth O'Connor, *Call to Commitment* (New York: Harper & Row, Publishers, Inc., 1963).

The LORD says, "I am making a new earth and new heavens. The events of the past will be completely forgotten. Be glad and rejoice forever in what I create. The new Jerusalem I make will be full of joy, and her people will be happy. I myself will be filled with joy because of Jerusalem and her people. There will be no weeping there, no calling for help. Babies will no longer die in infancy. . . . Even before they finish praying to me, I will answer their prayers. Wolves and lambs will eat together; lions will eat straw, as cattle do, and snakes will no longer be dangerous. On Zion, my sacred hill, there will be nothing harmful or evil" (Isaiah 65:17-20, 24-25, TEV; see also Isaiah 58:6–8).

And listen to the prophet Micah:

> . . . the mountain where the temple
>   stands
>   will be the highest one of all
>   towering above all the hills.
> Many nations will come
>   streaming to it,
> . . . He will settle disputes among
>   the nations,
>   among the great powers
>   near and far.
> They will hammer their
>   swords into plows
>   and their spears into pruning
>   knives.
> Nations will never again go to
>   war,
>   never prepare for battle
>   again.
> —Micah 4:1, TEV

What are God's intentions for the human future? God's intentions are to bring about a new heaven and a new earth, a new mountain and a new city, in which God dwells in the midst of the people forever. God intends to create a new age of righteousness in which there is no more sin; a new age of justice in which there is no more oppression of the poor; a new age of peace in which the instruments of war are transformed into the implements of peace; a new age of wholeness in which blind see and lame walk; a new age of restoration in which creation itself is not destroyed but restored. It will be a kingdom of reconciliation, homecoming, and great joy.

And we are promised a celebration to end all celebrations on God's holy mountain. Listen to what God has promised,

And the LORD of hosts will prepare a lavish banquet for all peoples on this mountain:

A banquet of aged wine, choice pieces with marrow,
And refined, aged wine.
And on this mountain He will swallow up the covering which is
over all peoples,
Even the veil which is stretched over all nations.
He will swallow up death for all time,
And the Lord GOD will wipe tears away from all faces,
And He will remove the reproach of His people from all the earth;
For the LORD has spoken.
And it will be said in that day,
"Behold, this is our God for whom we have waited that He might
save us.
This is the LORD for whom we have waited;
Let us rejoice and be glad in His salvation."

—Isaiah 25:6-9

This is imagery that the black church may understand more fully than others, but it is time we all embrace these compelling images of God's promise for the human future.

It is clear throughout the Old Testament that the future of God will come through the initiative of God and the initiative of God alone. And that initiative is to be expressed through a Messiah,

"Behold My Servant, whom I uphold;
My chosen one *in whom* My soul delights.
I have put My Spirit upon Him;
He will bring forth justice to the nations.
"He will not cry or raise *His voice*,
Nor make his voice heard in the street.
"A bruised reed He will not break,
And a dimly burning wick He will not extinguish;
He will faithfully bring forth justice.
"He will not be disheartened or crushed,
Until He has established justice in the earth;
And the coastlands will wait expectantly for His law."

—Isaiah 42:1–4

Come with me to the New Testament. In light of all that we have read, I have a whole new understanding of who this Messiah is. Watch Jesus as he stands up in the synagogue in his hometown at the beginning of his ministry. From the scroll of Isaiah he reads aloud:

"The Spirit of the Lord is upon Me, because He has anointed Me to preach the gospel to the poor. He has sent Me to proclaim release to the captives, and recovery of sight to the blind, to set free those who are downtrodden, to proclaim the favorable year of the Lord." And He closed the book, and gave it back to the attendant, and sat down; and the eyes of all in the synagogue were fixed upon Him. And He began to say to them, "Today this Scripture has been fulfilled in your hearing" (Luke 4:18-21).

Jesus made a remarkable claim! John Howard Yoder reminds us that the passage Jesus read out of Isaiah is the passage in which God promises to fully bring Jubilee.[2] The Jews had never been very faithful about following God's principles of Jubilee. (Every fifty years they were required by God to free all slaves, forgive all debts, and return all land to its original owners.) But God promises in Isaiah 61 that there was a new day coming in which he would fully establish Jubilee in the land. The captives would be set free; the poor would hear good news; justice would come.

John Howard Yoder maintains that when Jesus declared, "Today this Scripture has been fulfilled in your hearing," he was saying that he was, in fact, the promised Jubilee of God. He was Jubilee made flesh. Jesus was good news to the poor not only because of his words of hope and his compassionate touch but also because he was the harbinger of a new age of justice for the poor and the powerless as Mary had prophesied (Luke 1:46-55).

Here we are presented with a whole new understanding of who Jesus is. He isn't just the full disclosure of God. He is certainly that. Jesus Christ, the one we have chosen to follow, is the very future of God.

Do you want to see the future of God? Watch Jesus as he touches that man who has never walked. Watch that man run down the street praising God. There's the future of God. Watch Jesus as he opens the eyes of the blind. There's the future of God. Watch him feed the hungry, set free the possessed, and forgive the sinner. There's the future of God. In the servant life, the sacrificial death, and victorious resurrection of Jesus Christ we are shown a glimpse of the very future of God.

Orlando Costas contends,

> In Jesus' life and ministry God discloses the content of his kingdom far more clearly, comprehensively and deeply than in the life and history of Israel. . . . The kingdom is an indication of God's transforming presence in history . . . of his determination to make "all things new" (Revelation 21:5). The kingdom of God stands for a new order of life: the new humanity and the new creation which have become possible through the death and resurrection of Jesus. This new order includes reconciliation with God, neighbor and nature, and, therefore, participation in a new world. It involves freedom from the power of sin and death, and consequently the strength to live for God and humanity. It encompasses the hope

---

[2]John Howard Yoder, *The Politics of Jesus* (Grand Rapids: William B. Eerdmans Publishing Company, 1972), pp. 34-39.

of a more just and peaceful moral order, and thus it is a call to vital engagement in the historical struggles for justice and peace.[3]

The Kingdom, the Character of God, and the Scope of Redemption

The more we understand God's intentions for the future, the more we understand both the character of God and the nature of redemption. Too many of us live as though we are practicing deists. We live as though God is out to lunch somewhere and is neither involved in nor has purpose for the world. The God of Abraham and Sarah, Isaac and Rebekah, Jacob and Rachel, is alive and well and *that* God is bringing a particular future into being. The activist God of the children of Israel is still acting in history with vision and power.

In Jesus Christ the activist vision of God "became flesh; he came to dwell among us, and we saw his glory, such glory as befits the Father's only Son, full of grace and truth" (John 1:14, NEB). The incarnation is the clearest expression of God's love for people and the world and of the determination to achieve divine intentions for that world. Fackre has written, "Incarnation is the enfleshment of the seeking vision of God, of the God with Shalom on his mind, with the intention of liberation and reconciliation in the divine heart."[4]

J. Deotis Roberts reminds us that "amidst all the abuses, exploitation and injustices so abundant in our midst, we have the assurance that the benevolent, provident God in whom we trust is loving, just and merciful and that all evidence to the contrary, this God who is Lord over life and Lord of history will have the last word."[5]

Not only has God acted aggressively in incarnation and not only will God act decisively in consummation, God is acting in our world today. As the Communion elements were passed in the final scene of the film "Places in the Heart," it was as though the scales fell from my eyes. I had watched the entire film as I am sure I observe most life around me, as an essentially secular story in which God is absent. As the bread and wine were passed in that small Baptist church, I suddenly realized that God had been there all the time.

---

[3]Orlando E. Costas, *The Integrity of Mission: The Inner Life and Outreach of the Church* (New York: Harper & Row, Publishers, Inc., 1979), p. 6.

[4]Gabriel Fackre, *The Christian Story* (Grand Rapids: William B. Eerdmans Publishing Company, 1978), p. 96.

[5]J. Deotis Roberts, "Black Consciousness in Theological Perspective," *In Quest for a Black Theology*, J. Gardiner and J. Roberts, ed. (Philadelphia: Pilgrim Press, 1971), p. 71.

God had been there in the acts of kindness, the quiet forgiveness, and the struggle for life and dignity.

What does all this mean for those of us who have chosen to be disciples? It means quite simply that God who breathed worlds into being, liberated the children of Israel, and reached out to us in love through Jesus Christ is still alive and well. It means that God is still acting in history—your history and mine as well as the history of our world.

At a conference on ministry to the global poor, a campus pastor at the University of Washington gave us his definition of doing development work among the poor. Bob Schmidt said that Christian development simply means "getting the barriers out of the way of the grace of God." That's it! Getting out of the way of the grace of God. That's what being a disciple is about. Getting out of the way of the grace of God in our lives, our churches, and our world so that God can fully and aggressively bring the kingdom into being "on earth as it is in heaven."

Not only does a clearer view of God's intentions help us to understand more fully his loving, acting character, it also helps us to understand a more biblical view of redemption. There are a number of Christians who see God's redemptive mission in very narrow terms. They view God's redemptive mission as simply the saving of disembodied souls here to go to a nonmaterial heaven out there. If the Scripture we have reviewed in this chapter is to be taken seriously, then clearly God intends to redeem us as whole persons—mind, body, soul, and spirit—to be a part of the new heaven and new earth.

In other words, the Bible seems to teach a much more compre-

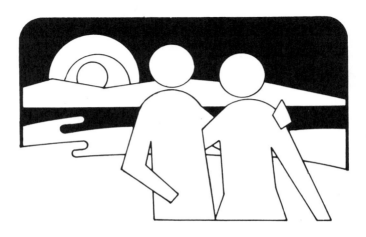

hensive view of redemption than is taught in many churches. God intends to create a new heaven and a new earth that is home not only to the redeemed, but home as well to a new age of righteousness, justice, peace, reconciliation, wholeness, and love. The scope of this redemptive design is broad indeed.

"Martin Luther King, Jr., was correct when he insisted that one cannot truly live until he has laid hold of something more precious than the present life. There is a sense in which life must receive its ultimate direction from beyond physical death if our life is to be rich and full."[6]

In this more comprehensive view of redemption God gives us direction that will make not only our own lives rich and full but the lives of others as well. A biblical view of God's kingdom provides us not only with hope but also with direction as disciples of Jesus Christ.

In other words, the more fully we understand God's intentions for the human future, the more fully we can be the presence of God's future today in life and action. As disciples of Jesus Christ we are called not to work for a little Christian gradualism, or to sit on our hands and wait for Jesus to come, nor to get our piece of the Great American Pie. We are called to work for a different vision. We are called as followers of Jesus to lay aside every lesser thing and seek first his kingdom of righteousness, justice, and peace with all of our lives.

J. Deotis Roberts is absolutely right when he says that our view of the future of God will either lead us to "withdrawal or to engagement."[7] If we follow the Jesus who announced the inbreaking of the kingdom of God, we are left with little choice. We are pressed into engagement with the most urgent issues of our time.

Now that we have some sense of God's intentions, of his redemptive designs, how should we then live? In light of this biblical view of the kingdom, what does it mean to be people of God? And what does it mean in our vocations, values, and lifestyles to seek first that kingdom?

Questions for Discussion

1. What are some nonbiblical images of the future to which people commit themselves?

2. What are God's intentions for the human future?

3. What are specific ways you can bring God's intentions for the future into being in your life as a disciple, in your church, community, and the larger world?

[6]J. Deotis Roberts, *A Black Political Theology* (Philadelphia: The Westminster Press, 1974), p. 183.
[7]*Ibid.*, p. 184.

3
CHAPTER

The People of God . . . The Presence of the Kingdom

There is no way we can follow Jesus alone. We can follow him only in community with others. Just spilling coffee on one another Sunday morning isn't community.

What is community then? What does following Jesus have to do with it? What precisely is the church? The intention of this chapter will be to enable us to understand (1) what is means to be the people of God; and (2) how our participation in community can enable us to be followers of Jesus Christ.

The Birth of a New Community

Too many Christians have confused buildings, bureaucracies, and institutions with the church. While it is possible for the church to gather in a building, the building is not the church. While it is often necessary for the people of God to have structure to accomplish their mission, institutional and bureaucratic structures are not the church. Even the weekly assembly of isolated individuals is not what it means to be the church. If we are to discover what it means to be the church, we must look to the Bible.

Remember, God's intentions from the beginning were to create a people for God's self . . . a people who were clearly different in their faith, culture, and values from those around them . . . a people who would faithfully follow their God.

Remember that the first thing Jesus did was to call people to himself: to form a new community. That new community of disciples was where he invested his greatest energy and vision. They shared celebrations and disappointments, times of struggle and times of prayer, miraculous acts of God and common meals. They lived with meager resources and shared with the poor whatever extra they received. They became bonded together as a new family and a foreshadow of God's new future.

Jesus challenged them to be a people apart. He taught them by word and deed to incarnate the right-side-up values of the kingdom of God. He prayed for them and for us.

> "I do not ask Thee to take them out of the world, but to keep them from the evil *one*. They are not of the world, even as I am not of the world. Sanctify them in the truth; Thy word is truth. . . . I do not ask in behalf of these alone, but for those who believe in Me through their word; that they may all be one; even as Thou, Father, *art* in Me, and I in Thee, that they also may be in Us; that the world may believe that Thou didst send Me" (John 17:15-21).

His prayer was powerfully answered. As the Spirit of God was poured out on that unlikely group in the upper room, they were galvanized into a new community. They were indeed united into one body even as Jesus had prayed. ". . . In this birth of the Church, the risen and ascended Lord takes to himself a body on earth opened by the Spirit to see the future. These are the dawn people, the children of light empowered to see the vision of God."[1] But they are not only empowered to see the vision of God, they are empowered to be the vision of God. Those earliest disciples and all of us who have said yes to his call are empowered to be the presence of God's kingdom in society, nothing less. Samuel Escobar declares, "God calls those who become his people to be a part of community. So the humanity that Christ is creating becomes visible communities that have the quality of life, that reflect Christ's example."[2] In reflecting Christ's example we are, of course, reflecting the values of God's new order.

Therefore, the church is principally the organic sacramental community of God reflecting the values of a new age, not simply a bureaucratic religious organization reflecting the dynamics of an institution. I think Howard Snyder sums it up best:

> . . . The church is a community or fellowship, a koinonia . . . if peoplehood underlines the continuity of God's plan from the Old

---

[1] Gabriel Fackre, *The Christian Story* (Grand Rapids: William B. Eerdmans Publishing Company, 1978), p. 150.

[2] Samuel Escobar, "Evangelism and Man's Search for Freedom, Justice and Fulfillment," *Let the Earth Hear His Voice* (Minneapolis: World Wide Publications, 1975), p. 312.

to New Testament, community calls attention to the 'new covenant,' the 'new wine,' the 'new thing' God did in the resurrection
of Jesus Christ and the Spirit's baptism at Pentecost. The emphasis
here is on the locality of the church in its intense, interactive common life. Seen as a charismatic organism, the church is the community of the Holy Spirit.[3]

In other words, the institutional structure is important to carry
out the programs of the church. But the essence of the church is to
be found in its organic and sacramental community life. The church
is intended to be a servant community in the world.

Creation of a New Culture

As disciples of Jesus Christ we are not just members of an institution, we are sisters and brothers sharing common life together by
the power of the Spirit of God. At the very center of our common
life is worship, and at the center of our worship is the preaching of
the Word and the sacraments. The character of that worship may
be different in black, Hispanic, and predominately white churches
but the ingredients are the same. God's grace comes to us through
the sacraments and Scriptures, and God's grace always changes us
when we respond in faith to the call of Christ.

Much has been written in the past few years about a secular threat
outside the church that threatens the life of the church. That threat
has been called "secular humanism." Those who favor abortion, are
sympathetic to gay rights, and are generally supportive of a liberal
political agenda are classified as "secular humanists."

The problem with this view of secularism is that it tends to exter-
nalize the secular, to put it outside of the church by defining the
viewpoint largely in political terms. This enables people who don't
support those "humanist agendas" to feel very self-righteous. Often
they fail to recognize the extent to which their own lives have been
secularized and their own churches captivated by the pagan values
of the dominant culture.

Many other Christians appear to be oblivious to the secular influ-
ences of contemporary society. Going to church is simply a part of
the larger cultural scene they have been conditioned to accept. This
group is almost totally unaware of its captivity.

However, both those who are concerned about "secular humanism" and those who seem not to be concerned about any form of
secularism fail to recognize the pervasive nature of the secular influence not just in society but in the church as well.

Research indicates that those of us who go to church are actually

[3]Howard A. Snyder, *The Problem of Wine Skins* (Downers Grove, Illinois: Inter-
Varsity Press, 1977), p. 59.

little different in our fundamental values from those who never darken the door of a church. Even though many of us have come to vital faith in Christ and our spiritual condition has been changed, too often our values have not changed.

In becoming Christian it appears that many of us have unquestionably attempted to layer our faith right over the top of the secular values with which we have been raised. We have simply accepted cultural expectations as largely unquestioned givens. For many, this business of following Christ seems to be placing a little "Jesus veneer" over middle- and upper middle-class lifestyles and their implicit values. That simply won't work.

Many of the values of American culture are diametrically opposed to the values of the servant Christ and his kingdom. For example, how can we buy into the cultural values of looking out for number one and seeking life, when Christ calls us to be willing to lose our lives? How can we put the cultural right of getting a piece of the Great American Pie at the center of our lives when Jesus calls us to be people for others?

How in the world can we place the secular values of materialism, individualism, and self-seeking at the center of life and follow the servant Jesus at the same time? The answer is: We can't.

Jim Wallis asserts, "Church historians may someday describe our period as the 'American Captivity of the Church.' It is no less real than the Babylonian Captivity in the history of Israel."[4] Our churches are captivated by the values of the secular culture and, for the most part, don't know it.

One has only to look at the early church to realize that those first disciples weren't simply putting a little religious veneer over the values of Roman culture. They realized that following Jesus meant not only having their spiritual condition changed but having their culture and values transformed as well. That first community of disciples didn't unquestioningly affirm the dominant culture; they challenged it at every turn. They not only refused to bow their knees to Caesar, they created a radical countercultural movement that turned the Roman world upside down.

That first countercultural Christian community shared meals from house to house, held all things in common, and broke down racial and cultural barriers that existed in Roman society. Michael Green concludes, "They made the grace of God credible by a society of love and mutual care which astonished the pagans and was recognized as something entirely new. It lent persuasiveness to their

[4]Jim Wallis, *The Call to Conversion: Recovering the Gospel for These Times* (New York: Harper & Row, Publishers, Inc.), p. 31.

claim that the New Age had dawned in Christ."[5] Wouldn't it be powerful if the American church were so astonishing and persuasive in its cultural witness that pagans today recognized that the kingdom of God had broken into their midst?

That early church wasn't simply accepting the Roman culture from nine to five during the week and then trying to get to a house church on the sabbath. To be a disciple of Jesus didn't mean just getting one's spiritual life worked out and viewing discipleship as the maintenance of that compartment of life while continuing the rest of life pretty much as before. No. Following Christ meant that his grace began changing his followers in every compartment of life. Far from living a life that quietly endorsed the dominant culture and its implicit values of prestige, power, and prosperity, the lives of those first disciples challenged the dominant culture.

Those first disciples understood that even as Christ incarnated the kingdom of God in his life, they were called as the body of Christ in society to be the presence of that kingdom in every dimension of life. For them:

> The message of the kingdom became more than an idea. A new human society had sprung up, and it looked very much like the new order to which the evangelists pointed. Here love was given daily expression; reconciliation was actually occurring. People were no longer divided into Jew and Gentile, slave and free, male and female. In this community the weak were protected, the stranger welcomed. People were healed, and the poor and the dispossessed were cared for and found justice. Everything was shared, joy abounded, and ordinary lives were filled with praise. Something was happening among these Christians that no one could deny. According to Tertullian, people looked at the early Christians and exclaimed, "See how they love one another!" The fervent character of Christian love not only bound them to one another; it also spilled over the boundaries of their own communities and extended to all in need. The economic sharing practiced by the early Christians, together with their generosity toward the poor, was one of the most evangelistic characteristics of their life.[6]

Here, then, is the first expression of God's kingdom in and through the body of Christ. When churches didn't reflect this level of commitment, the apostles or church leaders wrote strong letters to them, seeking to correct conduct that was not becoming of God's kingdom. These early Christian leaders seemed to understand more fully than we do today that following Jesus Christ means actively living all of

---

[5]Michael Green, *Evangelism in the Early Church* (Grand Rapids: William B. Eerdmans Publishing Company, 1970), p. 120.
   [6]Wallis, *The Call to Conversion*, pp. 15-16.

life under his lordship. It means placing his kingdom not at the periphery but at the very center of our lives, and it means actually becoming a foretaste of that kingdom in our culture to the extent that the Spirit fills us and grace transforms us. That transformation will affect both our personal and social ethics.

The church at its best has always been countercultural. The Franciscans, the Anabaptists, the Wesleyan lay movement, and the Quakers all marched to a very different drumbeat than the cultures around them. Consequently, they had a dramatic impact on those cultures for the kingdom.

When Graham Kerr (the former "Galloping Gourmet") and Treena Kerr became Christians nine years ago, it changed much more than their spiritual conditions. Graham immediately realized that his values and culture also had to be transformed. He said, "There is no way I can be the foremost example of American hedonism and follow Jesus." He and Treena gave up both the values and the lifestyles they had spent years building (the mansion, the yacht, and so forth). They now work for a Christian agency and are many times happier than before. They have discovered that the good life of God is the life given away.

Jacques Ellul is absolutely right when he asserts, "Israel and the church have never been efficacious except to the degree that the world has been unable to assimilate them."[7]

Tragically, the contemporary American church (unlike its first-century counterpart) is unable to challenge the values of American culture because it has indeed been largely assimilated by that culture. The pursuit of prosperity, prestige, and power is often as evident inside the church as outside. Walter Brueggemann charges that "this enculturation is . . . true across the spectrum of church life, both liberal and conservative."[8]

If the church has any hope at all of making a difference in society, it must first *be* a difference. We must pray for liberation from our idolatry of the values and preoccupations of our age so that we can be God's agents of change in this world.

The first call to disciples of Jesus Christ is not to proclamation or to social action. The first call is to incarnation. Until we begin to incarnate authentically the right-side-up values of Christ and his kingdom, we have nothing to proclaim and no basis on which to act.

In the *Upside-Down Kingdom* (which is an excellent study book),

---

[7]Jacques Ellul, *The Politics of God and the Politics of Man* (Grand Rapids: William B. Eerdmans Publishing Company, 1972), p. 141.

[8]Walter Brueggeman, *The Prophetic Imagination* (Philadelphia: Fortress Press, 1978), p. 11.

Donald Kraybill helps us to understand what it means to incarnate the values of the kingdom in culture. To incarnate is to live under the reign of Jesus Christ. It means to put others first; it means forgiving friends and loving enemies. It means putting spiritual and relational values ahead of our material security and personal affluence. To incarnate the kingdom means to go the second, third, and even the fourth mile, enduring personal insults, forgiving debts, giving to anyone who asks, and sharing resources with those in need. It is to exchange the pursuit of status and power for a life of servanthood and compassion. The values of Jesus are clearly countercultural in any society. They also seem terribly impractical.

However, John Alexander insists that they are not nearly as unthinkable or impractical as they may seem. "We just need to decide where we get our standards—from Jesus or our culture. If from Jesus, we will have to change in very extreme ways and it may seem costly. However, my . . . experience is that once I let go, following Jesus is tremendously liberating."[9]

Becoming the Community of God

Where does this transformation of our lives and values begin? It begins by letting go of our lives—in community with other sisters and brothers just like the first disciples did. We can be sure that God will aid us in "letting go" of all that holds us back and set us free to manifest the kingdom of love and joy.

The kind of radical change we are talking about here can happen

---

[9] Donald B. Kraybill, *The Upside-Down Kingdom* (Scottdale, Pennsylvania: Herald Press, 1978), p. 18.

only in community. To have genuine community there must be opportunity for knowing, vulnerability, accountability, and mutual support. Frankly, many churches are too large or too institutionalized to make possible anything more than superficial contact. Ron Sider states,

> I am thoroughly convinced, however, that the overwhelming majority of Western churches no longer understand or experience biblical koinonia to any significant degree. . . . the essence of Christian community is open accountability to and far-reaching liability for our sisters and brothers in the body of Christ. That means that our time, our money and our very selves are available to brothers and sisters.
>
> This kind of fellowship hardly ever happens in larger churches of one hundred or more persons. It requires small communities of believers like the early house churches.[10]

Of course God speaks to us, nourishes us, and changes us through Sunday worship, church school, midweek studies, and other programs in our local churches. To be serious disciples we must indeed be in "community." That means we need to be a part of groups that are small enough so that we can be known and intentional enough so that we can grow.

There are three different ways we can become a part of communities to facilitate our growth as disciples: (1) join or form a "house church," a small group or groups of families that meet together for worship and activity with little emphasis on traditional structures; (2) join or form small community groups within larger institutional churches; or (3) join or form a residential community with other believers.

For example, there is a network of small house churches in Minneapolis, Rochester, Indianapolis, and Seattle. They provide an alternative to the more highly structured and institutionalized churches. House churches tend to be more organic. Because of their size, people can be intimately known, loved, and supported in their discipleship.

Let's look at a house church in Seattle as a case study. It is composed of twenty-two people (including sixteen adults). They come together from 5 P.M. to 8:30 P.M. Sunday evening. They begin with a potluck dinner so that persons have an opportunity to get in touch with one another. There is a much higher commitment to one another than in a typical Sunday service. Members are open and vulnerable to one another. In that fellowship of trust, they have

---

[10]Ronald J. Sider, *Rich Christians in an Age of Hunger* (Downers Grove, Illinois: InterVarsity Press, second edition © 1984), p. 183. Used by permission of InterVarsity Press, Downers Grove, IL 60515.

helped one another through times of unemployment and marital crises . . . just like a family. Community at its best is always family.

After dinner the church plans for its mission efforts. In addition to being involved in individual ministries, members often do ministry together as an entire community. For example, they clean yards and paint houses for seniors who are unable to perform this upkeep for themselves.

One senior said that when he saw a bunch of kids and women coming to his house with paintbrushes he was "real worried." But the community painted the entire house in two days and, he commented, "It looked great."

After their evening planning time, members of the Seattle church share in corporate worship. Tom Nielson, one of the leaders, explained that the children and adults actually plan the worship time together. In fact, recently they participated in one worship time planned entirely by the children.

Because the house church doesn't have to support a building and the leaders are volunteers, overhead costs are low. Sometimes the church hires a Christian education specialist to work with the children. The church also helps members financially when someone is unemployed, but over 60 percent of the money contributed to the house church is invested in mission outside their fellowship. A share of the contributions goes to denominational mission; they support peace and justice efforts in the Seattle area as well.

Obviously a disciple in this community would not only find the love and support often missing in many churches, but also would be challenged to join others in becoming the countercultural presence of the kingdom in Seattle in mutual love and shared servanthood.

Most people who want to get serious about their discipleship don't have access to a house church, however. A more realistic option for most readers is simply to find or start a small community group in the church which you are already attending. Check with your pastor and see if there is a small group which has already started that you might join.

Failing that, see if you can find a few other people who want to get more serious about their discipleship. Plan to get together once a week. Decide what level of commitment you want to make to one another and to the group. Find enjoyable ways to get acquainted over meals or desserts. Decide how to use your time for Bible study, prayer, discipleship study, and mission planning.

Specifically plan ways to support and hold one another accountable in those areas in which God is challenging you to grow, not only in your spiritual life, but in transforming your values and lifestyle as well.

One way to work on cultural transformation is to study the Gospel of Luke and make four lists:

1. Before you begin the study, ask everyone to list cooperatively the values of the dominant culture . . . individualism, consumerism, privacy, and so forth.
2. Then ask everyone to list individually which of the values of the dominant culture are his or her values.
3. As you study through the Gospel of Luke, keep a running list of the values reflected in the life and teachings of Jesus, paying particular attention to the values of the kingdom of God.
4. Finally have everyone list individually which of the values of Christ and the kingdom are really his or her values.

What will happen in this type of process, of course, is that we will all wind up with two very different types of lists. Then we can invite God to help us begin finding new ways to flesh out the values of the kingdom in our own lives and families.

Some churches may want to create an organic network of small groups for their entire congregation. A suburban church in Portland, Oregon, broke its congregation down into this kind of small group structure. These groups meet every week. While they study the Bible, they are more than Bible study groups. While they pray, they are more than prayer meetings. Nuclear families, single-parent families, seniors, and divorced persons share a remarkable commitment to one another in these small groups.

These organic groups provide a place within an institutional church for people to know and care for one another and to work on their discipleship together. These groups are really extended families. One of the major thrusts of this small group program is to disciple all members for active ministry. In these groups, peoples' gifts, abilities, and vocations are identified and they are equipped to move outside the church in active ministry. Over 50 percent of the people in those small groups are now actively involved in mission outside their church.

Growing numbers of churches are creating organic home meeting networks to reestablish more intimate *koinonia* in the body and more serious discipleship in the laity. In a number of churches this type of program is also bringing renewal.

There are a few Christians like those in Sojourners (Washington, D.C.) and Reba Place (Chicago) who actually live in residential communities. They often share a common purse and assume total liability for one another in all areas of life. One of the major reasons that some choose this type of community is an attempt to give expression to the countercultural demands of the gospel in every area of life. They feel that an intentional Christian community provides them with the best opportunity to follow Christ faithfully.

It is in the context of Christian community that God meets us and begins to change us. God meets us through worship and the sacraments. God meets us in Christian education and Bible study groups. God seems to meet us most profoundly, however, in those groups within the body of Christ in which the commitment to the kingdom of God and one another is of the highest priority. In the first church, committed life in community wasn't optional; it was normative.

If we are to be followers of Jesus Christ in contemporary culture, we can't do it alone; we can do it only in concert with other brothers and sisters. We need to be very clear when we say "yes" to Jesus Christ and seek to follow him in community that it doesn't make us more righteous or spiritual than anyone else. It is only through grace that we find acceptance from God. If we follow Christ together, commit ourselves to *his* dream, and get out of the way of his grace, we have no idea of what he might do to manifest the kingdom of righteousness, justice, and peace in our midst.

"So the church is God's agent for establishing his Kingdom. It is the primary means by which he is accomplishing his reconciling purpose. Therefore, the Church is inseparable from God's cosmic design to sum up all things in Jesus Christ (Ephesians 1:10)—the essence and goal of the Kingdom."[11] As disciples of Christ we commit ourselves to the church and the mission of the church, manifesting the kingdom of God on earth. As God's grace begins to transform our lives and values, we need to explore how this transformation will influence our priorities, vocations, stewardship, and lifestyles.

Questions for Discussion

1. Why does God call us to be disciples in community with others?

2. In what specific ways are the values of the kingdom of God (that we are called to express in community) different from the values of the larger secular culture?

3. List specific practical ways in which you could become a part of an organic Christian community . . . seeking to be a difference and make a difference for the kingdom.

[11]Howard Snyder, *Community of the King* (Downers Grove, Illinois: Inter-Varsity Press, 1977), p. 13.

4
CHAPTER

Seeking First the Kingdom: Creative Lifestyles

If we indeed invite God to transform not only our spiritual lives but also our values and our culture, this decision is likely to change everything—our priorities, our schedules, even our lifestyles. That's another reason we need to be in community. We cannot make the changes God calls us to make as disciples without the support of others who are seeking first the kingdom.

The purpose of this chapter will be to outline what it means as disciples of Jesus Christ to seek first the kingdom of God in our stewardship, lifestyles, and priorities.

Seeking First the Kingdom in Whole-Life Stewardship

People, in the conventional view of Christian stewardship, typically give a percentage of their income, the tithe, and use the rest of their income on themselves. Many churches receive only 1 to 3 percent of a person's income. A few more evangelically oriented churches receive about 3 to 5 percent. Tragically, of the total amount the church receives, very little trickles out into any kind of ministry outside of the church building. Tony Campolo likens the church to an oil refinery that seems to need all the oil it refines just to keep its own machinery going.

But there are a few churches, such as the American Baptist house churches in Seattle, that give over 60 percent of their income to ministry outside their fellowship; and Trinity Presbyterian Church in Santa Ana, California, set the goal of giving over half of its budget to global mission.

A pastor of a small Lutheran church in Washington called the Lutheran World Relief office in New York to say that his church would be sending a check for $100,000. "We decided to borrow the money," he told the astonished chief administrator. "We figure we would be willing to do it for a church addition, so why not for the world's starving people?"

It's essential as we talk about this business of Christian stewardship that we keep the world and the growing number of starving people in the world in mind. It is estimated that there are some seventy million people on the threshold of starvation. The situation is particularly acute in Africa. We may be facing the worst famine of the century.

Beyond the specter of famine, there are some 800 million people around the globe living in absolute poverty; that is, they have an income of less than ninety dollars per person per year. These persons live in squalor at a subsistence level. Typically, half of their children don't survive to age five.

What has not been clear until now is that, according to David Barrett, of those 800 million who are living in absolute poverty, 195 million are our brothers and sisters in Christ. In other words, 195 million Christians are living in absolute poverty and their children are suffering from chronic malnutrition.[1]

Listen to Christ's words to the poor and hungry and to the affluent and well-fed: "Blessed *are* you who *are* poor, for yours is the kingdom of God. Blessed *are* you who hunger now, for you shall be satisfied. Blessed *are* you who weep now, for you shall laugh. . . . But woe to you who are rich, for you are receiving your comfort in full. Woe to you who are well-fed now, for you shall be hungry. Woe *to you* who laugh now, for you shall mourn and weep" (Luke 6:20-25).

In light of this Scripture, we need to ask what it means to be Christian stewards and earthkeepers in a world of growing need, malnutrition, and hunger in which our brothers and sisters are suffering. We need to reevaluate critically our conventional view of stewardship not only in light of growing world hunger but also in light of biblical teaching.

The conventional view of Christian stewardship is no longer adequate. Not only is it not responsive to the kind of world in which we live, but there is also growing evidence that the tithe itself isn't

[1] David Barrett, "Silver and Gold Have I None: Church of the Poor or Church of the Rich," *International Bulletin of Missionary Research*, vol. 7, no. 4 (October, 1983).

biblical. Of course, we all understand the Old Testament origins of the tithing principle. The problem is that there is evidence in the New Testament that the tithe was never normative for stewardship.

When Peter and Andrew followed Jesus, apparently they didn't even bother to sell their fishing boat. Zacchaeus gave half of his money to the poor and paid back four times over to anyone he had cheated. The rich young ruler was challenged to give all of his money away. Matthew left his lucrative tax collecting, never to return. Following Jesus in the New Testament was never a "10 percent commitment," but a whole-life proposition.

The problem with tithing is that it tends to fractionalize not only our view of stewardship, but also our view of Christian life and responsibility. Simply conforming to our own cultural living standards and values and giving out our leftovers isn't what we see going on in the New Testament. For those first believers, following Jesus was always a whole-life proposition including the ways in which they used their resources.

A growing number of New Testament scholars have come to the same conclusion as that of John Howard Yoder. The stewardship principle that seems to be operating in the New Testament isn't the tithe principle, but the Jubilee principle.

Not only did Christ inaugurate his ministry with the announcement that the Jubilee had come, but he and his disciples and, indeed, the early church seemed to live out the principles of the Jubilee in every aspect of life. They were not involved in simply giving 10 percent and doing what they wanted with the rest. Instead, they orchestrated their whole lives to maximize the greatest amount of time and money for the advance of God's kingdom. "Jesus makes it clear that He expects forgiven and converted people to live an upside-down economic life. He holds up the Jubilee model as the new way for His disciples. People on the way with Him respond financially to God's great love for them by sharing with those in need around them."[2]

The biblical premise for the Jubilee is that "the earth is the Lord's." Ron Sider points out, "As absolute owner, God places limitations on the acquistion and use of property. According to the Old Testament, 'the right to property was in principle subordinated to the obligation to care for the weaker members of society.'"[3] If we really believe the premise "the earth is the Lord's," then it is no longer a question of "how much of mine do I have to give up?" The question

[2]Donald B. Kraybill, *The Upside-Down Kingdom* (Scottdale, Pennsylvania: Herald Press, 1978), p. 113.
[3]Ronald J. Sider, *Rich Christians in an Age of Hunger* (Downers Grove, Illinois: Inter-Varsity Press, 1977), p. 103.

becomes "how much of God's do I keep?" in a world in which 195 million of my brothers and sisters in Christ and millions of others aren't making it.

That means before we add another parking lot to our church in Cleveland or Los Angeles, we need to ask if a church in Bolivia can afford a metal roof. Before we buy our recreational vehicles, we need to ask if Christian families in Haiti can keep their children fed.

As disciples of Jesus Christ we need a new biblical model of stewardship that is patterned after the Jubilee model of those first disciples and is responsive to desperate needs of our world today and tomorrow. In the first century of the church, following Christ meant much more than being spiritually converted. It affected all areas, including economics.

". . . massive economic sharing of the earliest Christian church is indisputable. 'Now the company of those who believed were of one heart and soul, and no one said that any of the things which he possessed was his own, but they had everything in common' (Acts 4:32). Everywhere in the early chapters of Acts, the evidence is abundant and unambiguous. . . . The early church continued the pattern of economic sharing practiced by Jesus."[4]

As we established in the last chapter, being a Christian in the early church meant having one's values and culture transformed. It meant becoming a part of a new community. And it meant a radical change of one's life priorities, use of resources, and lifestyle.

Following Jesus Christ is always a whole-life proposition. That's what it was for the first disciples and that's what is must be for us today. We don't necessarily have to give everything away (unless that is God's call for you); we do have to plan all of life to maximize the amount of time and money we have to invest in the work of God's kingdom.

At this point many people draw back because they assume that following Jesus means they have to give up a chunk of the "good life." Nothing could be further from the truth. The American Dream never was the "good life." How much we can accumulate in our garages, ring up in our charge accounts, and throw in our trash cans has nothing to do with happiness. Madison Avenue has sold us a bill of goods. Consumerism is not synonymous with happiness.

No people have ever consumed like Americans. Look at our mental health statistics, the amount of alcohol and other drugs we use, our suicide rate. We are apparently among the most unhappy people on this planet.

The journey toward a new biblical view of stewardship doesn't begin with cutting back or giving up a chunk of the "good life,"

[4] *Ibid.*, p. 88.

but in fundamentally redefining the "good life" itself. We must go back to the Bible and learn what Scripture teaches is the good life of God.

We are not primarily economic beings who will find our greatest fulfillment in ever more productive and ever more consumptive lifestyles. We aren't what we own. The Bible teaches that we are primarily spiritual and relational beings made in the image of our God, and we find our greatest fulfillment in reconciled relationships, Christian growth, and the surprising joy of giving life away.

Once we have begun to redefine biblically what the "good life" is, the next step isn't to subtract anything but to add to life new forms of Christian celebration. (One of the reasons the rest of the world may not take us seriously is that we are a little boring.)

We are called as disciples of Jesus Christ to be a people of unique celebration. We are not supposed to follow our culture mindlessly; we are supposed to be pacesetters. We are the ones who should teach the world to sing and dance and praise God. We should live as though Jesus has risen from the dead! We should be joy, hope, and celebration to a world that has lost hope.

All the imagery of the kingdom is imagery of celebration—the banquet, the wedding feast, the lost pearl, the harvest. We are called to be the celebrative presence of the kingdom of God in society. How do we do that? Where do we begin?

Some friends and I have been celebrating Jewish holidays for the past three years—Passover, Hanukkah, the Feast of Tabernacles. The last time we did the Feast of Tabernacles we had a whole houseful of people doing Jewish folk dancing, singing, and enjoying thoroughly the celebration.

Then, right there in the living room, we constructed a huge booth. (Historically, when Jews celebrated the Feast of Tabernacles they built special booths and lived in them for eight days.). We covered it with branches, bows, and berries. We jammed forty people into it. We ate falafal, praised God, and got in touch with a part of the Jewish heritage that had always been ours but which we had never claimed before.

We need to add new celebration to our lives from our Jewish past, our Christian past, our ethnic past, or to celebrate one another! We can even take biblical images of the kingdom such as the wedding feast or the harvest and create whole new Christian celebrations.

Once we have begun redefining the good life, adding to life new forms of celebration, then we come up against the stewardship question: "How much is enough?" How much floor space, wardrobe, transportation, recreation is enough for us?

The question can be answered by finding creative ways for stewardship of our whole lives not out of guilt but out of opportunity, to be more a part of what God is doing to change the world.

"The economic values of the kingdom are upside down in contrast to the dominant values of modern life . . . He . . . calls us to join the perpetual Jubilee of God's kingdom which even today looks upside down in the midst of contemporary culture."[5]

As disciples we can begin by discovering how God wants to use our lives and resources to make a difference for the kingdom. Then we can orchestrate our entire lives around that sense of ministry vocation.

For example, one couple felt called by God to help advance the work of the kingdom in Haiti. With a single income they devised a series of ways to make available financial resources for a project in Haiti about which they were concerned.

As newlyweds they rented a modest one-bedroom apartment and decided to use public transportation instead of buying a car. By so living, they saved 32 percent of their income, which they sent to the project in Haiti. That investment paid the full-time salary of one agriculturalist who worked with ten thousand people to help them become agriculturally self-reliant. That's whole-life stewardship.

Six students, upon graduation from Westmont College, Santa Barbara, moved to a poorer part of Oakland, California. God gave them a special concern for young people on the streets in that city. They found by living cooperatively in two rented flats that they could get by for roughly $250 per person per month for rent, food,

[5] Donald B. Kraybill, *The Upside-Down Kingdom* (Scottdale, Pennsylvania: Herald Press, 1978), p. 136.

and utilities. As a consequence of reducing their living costs, they didn't need full-time jobs to support themselves. Therefore they were able to invest more time in ministry. They went to First Baptist Church in downtown Oakland. Upon joining the church, they asked if they could re-open the church gym. They received permission and immediately had forty to sixty young people off the streets playing basketball.

Tom and Ida's kingdom vocation is to work with people who are handicapped. Instead of seeking paid professional positions to work with the handicapped, they chose an alternative pathway. They made a series of whole-life decisions that would enable them to carry out their vocation.

Their first decision was to build a house in the country. They constructed it with natural wood walls, cedar shakes, and 19R insulation for $10,000.

They built the house not just to save money but also to create a lifestyle without mortgage payments. They did that so a family of six could live comfortably for under $600 a month. Ida doesn't have to work outside her home at all; Tom only works half time.

They planned the life of their entire family so they have more time not only for one another but also for handicapped people who will move out to their community with them. As a consequence of being involved in whole-life stewardship, Tom and Ida will be able to minister to these people without cost to the state, church, or anyone else.

Whole-life stewardship is simply a matter of doing what a business person does every day of the week. In business the entire operation is designed to maximize the bottom line, which is, of course, profit. In whole-life stewardship a disciple designs his or her entire life to maximize the bottom line, which is freeing up time or resources for the work of God's kingdom.

Of course, the goal of whole-life stewardship is to seek first the kingdom of God. Jesus taught us, "Do not be anxious then, saying 'What shall we eat?' or 'What shall we drink?' or 'With what shall we clothe ourselves?' For all these things the Gentiles eagerly seek; for your heavenly Father knows that you need all these things. But seek first His kingdom and His righteousness; and all these things shall be added to you" (Matthew 6:31-33).

In other words, disciples of Jesus Christ are called to set aside every lesser agenda and with all of their lives to seek first the kingdom of righteousness, justice, peace, reconciliation, wholeness, and love. And if we do, we can count on God to meet our needs.

Seeking First the Kingdom Through Christian Time-Style

Whole-life stewardship begins in the place of prayer. Richard Foster notes, "Simplicity is an inward reality that results in an outward lifestyle."[6] Our "outward lifestyles" must be the reflection of the "inward reality." The indwelling presence of Christ is the reality which by the power of the Holy Spirit can transform our values, attitudes, and affections.

However, we cannot experience the indwelling presence of our Master unless we take time to be with him; and we won't take time to be with him if our schedules are so busy with everything else that we don't have any time left for prayer, meditation, and study.

One of the major areas of lifestyle struggle with which middle-class Christians wrestle is what I call "time-style." We book every single waking moment of our lives and then constantly complain about how busy we are as though someone else caused it. I have seen people who get a free evening immediately schedule something else. We live absolutely frenetic lives and have very little time for God or anyone else.

As we look at the time-style of the One we follow, we may see how far off the mark we are. His priorities were so different from ours. Where do we find Jesus in the New Testament? He is either with God or with people . . . that's all for which he had time. We either find him off in the mountains for extended times of prayer or we find him feeding or healing, relating to friends and followers, or proclaiming or confronting. If we are going to allow Jesus to change our lifestyles, we must begin by letting him change our time-styles.

I was in Haiti several years ago and one of the things I noticed was that my brothers and sisters there had time for relationships. They would simply drop by and spend a whole evening with friends. I came back to the United States determined to free one evening a week. I discovered it wasn't as hard as I thought. Now I've freed five evenings a week. It's a little bit like being out of debt. One can get used to it!

So the journey begins by clearing the deck. Find ways to free as much time as possible so that you really have time to invest in actually being a Christ follower.

Be ruthless. Cut everything out of your schedule that isn't absolutely essential. You may even drop some church committee meetings or commitments to organizations outside of the church. Then invite God to help you develop a new set of time-style priorities that reflect God's priorities.

Begin with setting aside time to be with God. You need to do this based on your life rhythms and your own situation. Some find that a time in the morning before work or before the family gets

[6]Richard Foster, *Celebration of Discipline: Path to Spiritual Growth* (New York: Harper & Row, Publishers, Inc., 1978), p. 75.

up is best. Others use their lunch hour for prayer and study. Many find that a time in the evening is best. I would suggest you not only find a time and stick to it, but a place as well. It helps to have a secluded place that is set aside just for encountering God, whether it's a quiet room, a park, or alone in your car.

Develop variety and imagination in how you use that time. Include reading the Bible and occasionally try a Bible study. Some find it valuable to memorize Scripture. Many of us, influenced by Richard Foster's book *The Celebration of Discipline,* are learning to meditate on Scripture.

For example, read a passage in the New Testament such as the scene at the empty tomb. Then spend a period of time meditating on it, picturing yourself as one of those first witnesses. You may be surprised at what God will teach you through such a process.

It is important that you also set aside time for other forms of meditation, contemplation, and prayer. Our lives often crowd into our consciousness, making prayer very difficult for us. Someone told me I had "the worst case of brain fever" he had ever seen. And he was right. As soon as I started to pray, my mind would almost explode with an incredible array of problems, ideas, uncompleted assignments, worries, resentments, fears, and so forth.

It took me a while to learn how to "center down," to focus my full attention on God and prayer. I found an ancient Christian technique of meditation which helped me. I settled into a comfortable relaxed prayer posture and began to breathe deeply. As I exhaled, I consciously breathed out all the negative feelings inside me—one at a time. I breathed out the worries and anxieties and I breathed out the distracting ideas.

Then I breathed in the peace of God, the presence of God, and slowly learned to focus my attention almost exclusively on God. We Protestants have much to learn from the Roman Catholics about what they call spiritual disciplines.

Too often our prayer lives are just another way of focusing on problems, worrying in the presence of God. While we should bring our petitions, problems, and needs before God, as disciples our prayer lives need to be more than that.

Experiment with using hymns, gospel songs, and Christian poetry to make your prayer time a season of praise and thanksgiving. Try the *Book of Common Prayer* or books of prayers written by men and women who knew God intimately. Often these will enrich the character of prayer life.

Try simply waiting before God in silence, listening for God's word and affirmation to you. I find that having a prayer list that varies from day to day broadens my focus in intercession for others. It helps me to focus beyond my own problems and begin praying for specific needs in both the church and the world.

One dimension of spiritual life that has become absolutely essential in my own disciplines is journal work. There are many different ways to use a journal to facilitate Christian growth. Once or twice a week I write down what I am learning from God, areas of failure, and areas of breakthrough. Over time I get a much better profile of the growth and setbacks in my life. Keeping a journal provides yet another vehicle for communicating with God.

Periodic retreat is also very helpful. Some go on a one- to three-day retreat once a year. Others do it twice a year or quarterly. Try to find a Sunday or Saturday once or twice a year to get completely away by yourself. There are many retreat facilities that are open to all denominations, or go to a cabin or park.

Take your Bible, journal, and study resources and set aside a day or two simply to be away with God. You may also want to fast. In any case, leave responsibilities and emotional pressures behind and try to hear afresh all the ways God wants to transform you into the kingdom person you can be.

What happens for me during these times of retreat is that God really sharpens the call on my life. I come back with a new sense of goals for my spiritual development, my community life, my relationships, my ministry vocation, and my occupation.

Then I redo my schedule to reflect more fully what I sense are God's priorities for my life. I then find it helpful to take some time each Sunday to evaluate how effectively I am responding to God's call in my weekly schedule and in my personal relationships.

It's important to remember what Richard Foster has written about the spiritual disciplines. Becoming more serious in our devotional lives in no way makes us more spiritual; it simply puts us in a place where it may be easier for God's grace to touch us.

After we have found time in our lives for a regular encounter with God, we need to find time to be in community with the body of Christ. As was indicated in the last chapter, Sunday morning is not enough. We need some regular time, probably one evening a week, with a small group of sisters and brothers in our church with whom God has called us into community. This weekly time of community needs to be stringently protected from other activities if it is to have the significance it deserves.

We also need to provide much more time in our lives for celebration and relationship as our Hispanic brothers and sisters do. Not only do we need more creative time with family and friends but we need more time to share our lives and homes with those on the fringes as Christ did. Celebration and festivity need to be much more a part of our lives if we are to be the living evidence that God's kingdom has broken into the world.

Just about everyone of us can, as we rework our schedules, find regular time every week to care about someone else. Those first disciples, like their Master, were able to find time in their lives for others. I suspect that most of us could find two to four hours a week to minister to someone else. We will develop this theme more in the next chapter.

Finally, in addition to participating faithfully in corporate worship, we need to decide how much time we can invest in the institutional structure of the church. We need to do a much better job of drawing people at the edges of the congregation into these responsibilities so that a committed core group doesn't burn out. We also need to evaluate our various committees and programs to determine if they are really essential to the life and mission of our churches.[7]

Once we rework our schedules in a way that enables us to live out more authentically the values of the kingdom and to participate more consistently in spiritual disciplines, community, and ministry, our discipleship will begin to take exciting new form and substance.

Donald Kraybill affirms, "When the kingdom is our treasure, we switch from hoarding to giving. When we focus completely on the kingdom and liberally share our wealth, we not only restore and liberate the poor but also ourselves![8] God always gives us more than we give God. That's the surprising nature of God's kingdom.

What impact does all of this discussion on transformation of our values, changing our lifestyles, and altering our schedules have on our jobs, our professional direction, and on our ministries?

Questions for Discussion

1. What are some examples of whole-life stewardship that you find in the New Testament?

2. What are some creative new ways you could add more celebration to your life?

3. What are some creative new ways you can use your time or resources differently to express more fully the kingdom of God?

---

[7]Two books in particular could assist a church seeking to do such evaluation. They are *Discover Your Gifts Workbook* and *Planning Growth in Your Church*, by Duncan McIntosh and Richard E. Rusbuldt.

[8]Donald B. Kraybill, *The Upside-Down Kingdom* (Scottdale, Pennsylvania: Herald Press, 1978), p. 116.

5
CHAPTER

Seeking First
the Kingdom: Creative
Vocations

One of the things that seems to be clear about the early Christians is they all appear to be participants in active ministry for the kingdom. There's no "professionals–laity" distinction.

Somehow over the centuries we have developed a two-tier system of Christian responsibility. It's what I call "surrogate servanthood." That is, we have hired clergy and other professional ministry staff to minister in our stead. The laity may be involved in committee meetings, occasional volunteer activities, and sporadic philanthropy, but this business of really getting involved in the ministry of Jesus in the world—that's what "professional clergy" do.

Discovering a Biblical View of Christian Vocation

In this chapter we will attempt to recover a biblical view of Christian vocation for disciples of Jesus Christ. We will attempt not only to clarify a biblical view of vocation but also to provide a range of models being used by God to make a difference in the world for the sake of the kingdom.

In this chapter we want to make a very clear distinction between ministry vocation and economic occupation. They can, of course, be the same. But I differ with those who state all jobs are automatically ministry vocation. This viewpoint originates from sixteenth-century reformers who taught that all jobs should be done to the glory of God. Certainly all human activity should be done to the glory of God and all kinds of work have dignity, but that doesn't necessarily mean that all occupations are automatically ministry vocations.

Some jobs are pointless. Some jobs are destructive of the environment and cause suffering among the poor. Still other jobs clearly are working to advance what we understand to be the purposes of God's kingdom.

One of the things that is patently evident in the New Testament is that people often quit jobs to follow Christ in their ministry vocation. There is absolutely nothing wrong with fishing as an occupation but Jesus called four fishermen to new vocations. Over and over, those who follow Christ not only leave their homes and change their lifestyles but frequently they also quit their jobs to fulfill their vocations!

For example, Jesus saw ". . . a tax gatherer, Levi by name, at his seat in the custom-house, and said to him, 'Follow me'; and he rose to his feet, left everything behind, and followed him" (Luke 5:27-28, NEB).

Paul took part-time jobs making tents to make it possible for him to support his vocation. This is not to suggest that all disciples today will quit their jobs or find part-time employment to support their ministry. Undoubtedly some will. Numbers of Christians today are altering their occupational lives to give primacy to their ministry vocations.

Yet I have found in the churches with which I work that over 85 percent of the congregation is "in the bleachers" and not involved in ministry with anyone. Some feel it's the responsibility of the professional church staff. Many feel one can be a committed church person simply by serving on committees. Still others seem to feel a little word for Jesus on the job is all that is required.

If we are to become serious followers of the Master, we need to discover how Jesus wants to use our lives intentionally to change the world. Therefore, we will define ministry vocation to mean discovering how we can use our lives and gifts to advance the kingdom in response to the needs in our world today and tomorrow.

However, before we act out our vocations in mission and ministry, we need to be sure we are struggling to incarnate the values of the kingdom in our lives (as discussed in chapter 4). The first call of the kingdom is to allow God to begin transforming us so that we reflect something of God's love and joy and the "right-side-up values" of God's new order.

For persons living in nursing homes, raising small children, or involved for a time in impossible work schedules, ministry vocation may be limited to the living out of faith in daily lives. Most of us, however, can find a way to move beyond an incarnational witness to an active witness. Most of us could find one evening a week to minister to others.

My grandmother was able to make this transition. She exuded the love and joy of God everywhere she went. In her declining years she was placed in a nursing home, a place where she really didn't want to be. Yet, instead of puzzling about why God had allowed her to wind up there, she did what she had always done. She focused on the needs of others and found a new vocation. She spent the better part of every day reading Scripture and stories to others in the nursing home who felt abandoned.

Finding God's Vocational Call

The only way we can understand God's vocation for our lives is to understand God's intentions for the world. God loves the world. Through the death and resurrection of Jesus Christ, God is actively redeeming people and transforming the world.

God intends to create a new heaven and a new earth, a new society of righteousness, justice, peace, reconciliation, wholeness, and love. The Bible teaches that God's kingdom is both present and coming, both now and "not yet."

God has chosen to do this work through women and men. We are to manifest the kingdom in partial ways now in anticipation of that day when Christ returns and the kingdom comes in its fullness. God has chosen to work through your life and mine to bring about righteousness, justice, peace, reconciliation, wholeness, and love in partnership with other members of the body of Christ.

In other words, when Jesus Christ charges us as disciples to "set your mind on God's kingdom and his justice before everything else," he means it. And he assures us that "all the rest will come to you as well" (Matthew 6:33, NEB).

If we are to take Jesus seriously, then he challenges us to set aside everything of lesser importance—family, profession, the pursuit of affluence, status, or power, and seek first the kingdom. We are to put the kingdom at the very center of our lives and, like those first-century followers, orchestrate the rest of life around it.

For some it will mean freeing one evening a week to work with handicapped children. For others it might mean reducing their standards of living and working half-time to have twenty hours a week free for ministry vocation. For still others it might indeed mean quitting jobs to pursue ministry vocations in different ways.

Models of Disciples in Ministry

Obviously for the seven people from the Ohio church who were mentioned in the Introduction, serving in Haiti for two years meant

quitting some jobs back home. It meant taking serious risks for the kingdom.

For a group of young people at a church in White Plains, New York, discipleship began with a visit to a prison. Now twenty-six young people and adults in the congregation are visiting inmates regularly. They are helping them plan to find jobs and be reunited with families when they are released. One prisoner wrote "thank you for coming to see me and also thank you for your true concern for me." That's the kingdom at work.

For Gordon and Brad, father and son from Paoli, Pennsylvania, God's vocational call on their lives was to be witnesses for peace. Recently they were among forty-five anti-nuclear protestors arrested at the General Electric Space Division. Gordon said, "I believe that making nuclear weapons of any kind is a crime against humanity and these weapons ought to be abolished."

Daniel and Caroline were working with international students. Convinced they had to have two full-time incomes to survive, the best they could do was to free one evening a week for ministry. Then, as they prayed about their further ministry, they felt they weren't fully honoring God's call on their lives, so they did something very radical. Dan quit his job as a math teacher and Caroline quit her job as a secretary. They found by moving into a Christian community that they could get by on one-half of one income instead of two full-time incomes. They took half-time jobs in their church as administrators (ten hours a week each). Now instead of a few hours a week working among internationals, Dan and Caroline each have thirty hours a week to give. God is richly blessing their ministry and their lives.

What they have done is to put God's call at the center of their lives and designed the rest of their lives around it. That's whole-life stewardship, disciples responding to their ministry vocation.

Mark found a way to follow God's call by allowing God to transform his job as an attorney into a ministry vocation. He realized his legal work was a very secular part of his life. As he prayed about it, he felt impressed to try a new approach. He decided to lock his office door every morning and spend the first hour in prayer for his clients. He reports amazing results. He finds he not only relates to his clients with a new level of sensitivity but also that God has begun using him in remarkable new ways as an agent of reconciliation and spiritual counselor to those with whom he works.

Al felt that God had called him into engineering. When he completed his degree at the University of Washington, he went job hunting. He turned down a job at Boeing making nuclear missiles. That didn't seem to him to be consistent with his sense of calling. He finally took a job redesigning cardiology equipment.

Then one day Al visited an institution for children with cerebral palsy, children trapped in bodies that don't move or communicate very well. Suddenly, Al realized what he had to do. He has now gone to graduate school to learn how to use engineering design to help handicapped kids. He has discovered that God's vocation for him is to be an agent of wholeness for children.

Sherman Frost, of Granville, Ohio, found his vocation in his own unemployment. After two years of unemployment he was experiencing what he described as "hopeless desperation."

He and an unemployed friend talked to pastor George Williamson about how they might help themselves and others facing the depression and frustration of unemployment. The Employment Initiative Cooperative was born out of that conversation.

The cooperative is based on the self-help principles of Alcoholics Anonymous. In addition to discussion of feelings and attitudes related to unemployment, the group offers its members temporary child care during job search efforts, assistance with transportation for job search efforts and interviews, information about the services of public employment and unemployment agencies, assistance in improving skills in resumé writing and interview techniques, and the pooling of job referrals. Sherman Frost learned that God can transform even our most frustrating situations into ministry vocations.

Discovering Vocational Calling for the Church

While speaking at a suburban church, I mentioned the need for churches to create ministry opportunities for whole families so they could be families for others. I returned to that church some weeks later. A woman approached me and said, "I am doing it—what you suggested. I am helping with household chores for seniors who are bedfast. I take my two pre-schoolers with me and they don't just watch Mom work; they are right down there on the floor with me scrubbing the tile."

Wouldn't it be marvelous if churches created ministry opportunities for whole families? We would raise young people who know more about servanthood and less about narcissism.

This will be no small task, however. Another church I visited in the Northwest has fantastic programs for its members but virtually no ministry outside its building. In light of the escalating challenges of the eighties and nineties, that kind of self-involved Christianity is simply irresponsible. Too many of our churches have settled for simply maintaining a certain kind of culture for people who bring their children to that particular church.

Sometimes the last thing we expect is for the community around the church building to change because the church is there. Our churches have become cultural maintenance stations instead of agents of radical change. Clearly, the church in the book of Acts wasn't maintaining anything; it was used by the power of God's Spirit to turn the Roman world upside down.

Therefore, it isn't enough for the church to enable individual disciples to discover their mission and ministry vocations. The church must discover its vocation, too. The local church needs to set aside its self-involved agenda and seek first God's kingdom of righteousness, justice, and peace every bit as much as its members. Churches need to set a goal of freeing 50 percent of their resources and 50 percent of their members' time for mission outside the building if we are going to be serious about the work of God in the world.

In the wake of further government cutbacks to those in need, handouts are no longer enough. We need new ministries that will empower the poor, that will help people to help themselves. We need to go beyond food pantries and clothing bins. We need local churches to start small businesses, job training programs, urban agriculture projects, and self-help health care centers.

For example, a Presbyterian church in Seattle working with Laotian refugees helped them start a church and was giving them free food and financial support while they looked unsuccessfully for jobs. (Laotian refugees are not usually accustomed to an urban economy.) Finally one of the Laotian men said, "I want to farm." That had not occurred to anyone in the church. The church leased twenty acres from the county and got an agricultural specialist to teach the refugees how to plant seeds in that area. (If you plant seeds too deep in Seattle, you will never see them again!)

The church then helped them develop a marketing strategy to

grocery stores and restaurants in the Seattle area. The Laotian women also did beautiful embroidery which was marketed to art museums in the United States.

In two years fifty Laotian refugees not only can have their own church, they can also be self-reliant economically because a church cared enough not simply to give them a handout but a "hand-up" toward dignity and self-reliance.

In the eighties and nineties we need hundreds of churches to commit themselves to seek first God's kingdom in a world of exploding need; churches that place mission above maintenance; churches, determined by the power of God's Spirit, to make a difference in their communities; churches that will minister in evangelism as well as social action and systemic change to empower those in need.

Hearing the Call

How can individuals and churches discover God's ministry vocation for their lives and congregations? How can they know what God wants them to do?

When speaking at Christian colleges I often say, half facetiously, that the most popular game on Christian campuses is called "finding the ideal, perfect, private will of God for my life." This game typically begins with the question: "What do I want and what will God let me have?"

For example, a young man nearing graduation interviews for a high-paying job and begins negotiating with God, "Dear God, if I could get the job, I could afford the apartment, the Porsche, and the trip to Europe. Just this one job, God. Please?"

The last question that is asked, if it is asked at all, is the question of ministry vocation. The pastor comes up to the young man and asks, "Now that you are out of school, do you think you could usher once in a while?" The response is, "You can count on me, Pastor. If the slopes aren't good, I'll be there."

One can't find God's will simply by asking the American Dream question: "What do I want and what will God let me have?" The only way we can find ministry vocations for our lives and congregations is by asking, "What does God want?" And, "How can I or my church be a part of what God is doing in the world?"

If we are disciples of Jesus Christ, individually and corporately, then we are obligated to put his kingdom at the center of our lives and congregations. Not only will this decision transform our values and lifestyles but it will also provide an integrating focus that gives life meaning and zest.

The Lord of history invites us to join together not with part of our lives but with all of our lives in the adventure and celebration of seeing this world changed. That invitation moves beyond economic accumulation and cultural maintenance to give challenging purpose to our individual and corporate discipleship.

Listen to Ron Sider's call to significant living: "If at this moment in history a few million Christians in affluent nations dare to join hands with the poor around the world, we will decisively influence the course of world history. Together we must strive to be a biblical people ready to follow wherever Scripture leads. We must pray for courage to bear any cross, suffer any loss and joyfully embrace any sacrifice that biblical faith requires. . . . We know that our Lord Jesus is alive! We know that the decisive victory over sin and death has occurred. We know that the Sovereign of the Universe wills an end to hunger, injustice and oppression. The resurrection of Jesus is our guarantee that, in spite of the massive evil that sometimes almost overwhelms us, the final victory will surely come. Secure on that solid rock, we will plunge into this unjust world, changing now all we can and knowing that the Risen King will complete the victory at his glorious return."[1]

Questions for Discussion

1. What was the difference between economic occupations and Christian ministry in the New Testament?

[1] Ronald J. Sider, *Rich Christians in an Age of Hunger* (Downers Grove, Illinois: Inter-Varsity Press, 1977), p. 224.

2. What are some creative new ways you could use your gifts, through your occupation or during your leisure time, to make a difference for the kingdom?

3. What are some imaginative new ways your church could invest more of its collective time, facilities, or resources in active ministry in community?

6
CHAPTER

Seeking First
the Kingdom: Making
Disciples

Thus far in this book we have discovered that if we take seriously the call of Christ, he will not only begin transforming our spiritual condition, he will also begin transforming our entire lives in community with other sisters and brothers. And he will give us new ministry vocations that will be at the very center of our lives. We will discover the satisfaction of manifesting the kingdom in the world.

Following Jesus in Disciple-Making

Our calling as disciples, however, doesn't end there. Listen to the commissioning words of Jesus after his resurrection: "The eleven disciples made their way to Galilee, to the mountain where Jesus had told them to meet him. When they saw him, they fell prostrate before him, though some were doubtful. Jesus then came up and spoke to them. He said: 'Full authority in heaven and on earth has been committed to me. Go forth therefore and make all nations my disciples; baptize men everywhere in the name of the Father and the Son and the Holy Spirit, and teach them to observe all that I have commanded you. And be assured, I am with you always, to the end of time'" (Matthew 28:16-20, NEB).

For too long this passage has been understood principally as a call to evangelism. New Testament scholars tell us that it principally is a call to disciple-making. Therefore, those of us who have chosen to respond affirmatively to the call of Christ on our lives have also been called to be disciple makers.

The purpose of this chapter will be to understand what it means to be a disciple maker and to discover specific ways we can disciple others who choose to follow Jesus.

Orlando Costas writes: "The reappearance of the concept of disciple-making as a central thrust of Christian ministry is a rediscovery of a basic New Testament concern."[1]

What does it mean to be a maker of disciples? What is involved? How do we go about it? As people come to faith in Jesus Christ and join a church, they must still decide how they want to follow Christ in discipleship.

It is important to emphasize here that neither the Christian who is struggling with radical discipleship or the Christian who settles for a more conventional notion of Christianity is any more or less righteous. Only the grace of God makes us righteous, nothing that we do through our own activity. Having said that, those of us who have decided to follow Christ in a more radical way are still obligated not only to call others to join us but also to help prepare them for the journey.

The journey begins, of course, when an individual comes to vital faith in Jesus Christ. The sooner that a new convert can begin developing the disciplines of Christian life, the better. Often it is very difficult for a Christian who has been in a conventional church for a long time to consider seriously the life changes that discipleship requires. However, for those who are motivated, whether new converts or established Christians, there are no limits to what God can do with their lives.

We should be very candid with people concerning the possible consequences on their lives of following Christ's call. We need to tell them that serious discipleship is likely not only to affect their spiritual lives, but also to challenge their values, upset their schedules, and alter their lifestyles. The possible positive benefits should also be mentioned.

Not all who have begun the journey of discipleship in their own lives should assume full-time vocational responsibility to be disciple makers. For those who do have both the calling and the gifts to play this vital role in the life of the church there are essentially four approaches to disciple making: (1) personal discipling, (2) household discipling, (3) small group discipling, and (4) church discipling.

---

[1] Orlando E. Costas, *The Integrity of Mission: The Inner Life and Outreach of the Church* (New York: Harper & Row, Publishers, Inc., 1979), p. 13.

Personal Discipling

Jesus' call to follow is always a personal call. He spent personal time with many of his disciples. Often there is a direct correlation between the personal investment of the discipler and the disciple's growth. For that reason, if you have the responsibility to disciple people in your church, you should seriously consider the more intimate person-to-person approach.

Dawson Trottman started an organization called Navigators, entirely based on a person-to-person discipling process. It flourished rapidly because Christians invested themselves so totally in the lives of others, helping them get into a serious and systematic program of devotion and Bible study.

Personal discipleship has been around as long as the church itself. In some churches discipling is called "spiritual direction" and the one who does it is a "spiritual director." In the Celtic Church in England the spiritual director was called a "soul-friend." "Anyone without a soul-friend was essentially a counselor and guide . . . often the soul-friend was a layman or a laywoman."[2]

A surprising number of Christians in the Middle Ages had spiritual directors or soul-friends to help them grow in their faith. In the fifteenth century St. Antonius wrote: "To assist at the love of God and devotion, to possess peace . . . it is useful and necessary to have a spiritual guide to whom you can report at all times your conduct and your failings that he may help and counsel you and allow you to know your state from hour to hour."[3]

There is a remarkable and growing interest today not only in the spiritual disciplines but also in spiritual directors, and an unusual number of Protestants who are very serious about their spiritual growth are finding spiritual directors to help them in their journeys.

Whether you call it spiritual direction or discipling, there are clear advantages to mature Christians working with disciples on a personal basis. I suggest that your church explore some of the systematic methodologies used by your denomination.

Household Discipling

"Jesus and the apostles often presented the gospel to a whole family or household together. The Scripture records that . . . a household would turn to the Lord Jesus at almost the same time."[4]

In middle-class white culture there is heavy emphasis on individ-

[2]Kenneth Leech, *Soul Friend: The Practice of Christian Spirituality* (New York: Harper & Row, Publishers, Inc., 1977), p. 50.
[3]*Ibid.* p. 57.
[4]Vergil Gerber, ed., *Discipling Through Theological Education by Extension* (Chicago: Moody Press, 1980), p. 51.

ual life, individual truth, and individual evangelism. For example, we try to "reach teens for Christ" individually. In many other cultures, including Hispanic culture, that doesn't work very well because decisions are often made by families, not individuals. Therefore, perhaps we would be better advised in some situations to disciple whole families or households instead of individuals. Churches embarking on household discipling programs could use the help of their Christian education specialists and denominational cross-generational discipling materials.

Small Group Discipling

As suggested earlier in the book, every serious Christian should be involved in a committed community group whether it is a Bible study, lay witness, or less conventional group. Probably Christ's major work in discipling took place in his small community with the twelve. If an institutional church developed a network of small organic groups for its members, that would in many ways be the best place to prepare disciples. West Hills Covenant Church in Portland has developed a way both to disciple its people and to equip them for ministry through small community groups. This approach to disciple-making is renewing the church.

The advantage of discipling in a small group is that believers are working together in a context of growing trust, community, vulnerability, and accountability. The early church was really a discipling community and sets the model for the church today.

Church Discipling

In some ways the easiest approach for churches to disciple their members is in a formal church education program. However, I am

not sure it is always best. This type of program tends to take on the more structured and sometimes impersonal character of other institutional programs. In that kind of format, discipleship is likely to take the form of a detached academic study. It could thus be more difficult to secure a high level of commitment to a radically biblical form of discipleship. However, this approach may be the only one some churches can use.

Jesus, the Master Teacher

If we are to understand anything of the pedagogy of Jesus, we need to remind ourselves of his background and distinctive personhood. We often seem to find him alone, a person of the mountains and a person of the deserts. Retreat, prayer, and meditation were very much at the center of the life of this Master Teacher. His remarkable intimacy with and dependence on God set him apart from other people and other teachers.

Jesus was also a person of study. We know less about this part of his background since he was apparently self-educated and didn't attend rabbinic schools, but even as a child of twelve he was remarkably advanced in his education. Remember when his parents couldn't find him in the caravan and they returned to Jerusalem? ". . . and after three days they found him sitting in the temple surrounded by the teachers, listening to them and putting questions; and all who heard him were amazed at his intelligence and the answers he gave. . . . As Jesus grew up he advanced in wisdom and in favour with God and men" (Luke 2:46-47, 52, NEB).

His father was a carpenter and evidence suggests that Jesus was too. He knew how to work with his hands. He knew the experience of a hard day's work and the satisfaction of fashioning wood into something of beauty and usefulness.

Not only was this teacher a person of the mountains, the study, and the shop, he was also a person of the streets. He knew people—all kinds of people. As a child in Nazareth he must have spent a great deal of time with people.

For after he read from Isaiah 61 in his hometown synagogue at the inauguration of his ministry, "There was a general stir of admiration; they were surprised that words of such grace should fall from his lips. 'Is not this Joseph's son?' they asked" (Luke 4:22, NEB). They knew Jesus as Joseph's son, though they were obviously surprised that this young man, whom they had seen in the streets and markets of Nazareth, had such an evident gift of teaching.

This Jesus was thoroughly Jewish. He was thoroughly immersed in first-century Jewish culture and couldn't have been unfamiliar with the encroaching culture of Rome. Yet somehow he was a man apart. Chronically, he seemed to find himself in hot water with those who saw themselves as the definitive interpreters of faith or culture.

Clearly he respected the tradition of his father and mother. He respected the synagogue. He followed the law of Moses even though he frequently violated interpretations of that law and went against convention.

Lawyers and Pharisees listened to Jesus teach in the synagogues and watched to see if he would heal on the sabbath. "He knew what was in their minds and said to the man with the withered arm, 'Get up and stand out here.' So he got up and stood there. Then Jesus said to them, 'I put the question to you: is it permitted to do good or to do evil on the Sabbath, to save life or to destroy it?' He looked round at them all and then said to the man, 'Stretch out your arm.' He did so, and his arm was restored. But they were beside themselves with anger, and began to discuss among themselves what they could do to Jesus" (Luke 6:8-11, NEB).

Of course they were angry. Jesus repeatedly exposed the hypocrisy of their legalism and convention and called people back to the values of love, justice, and faith. In his life, action, and teaching Jesus became so counter to the prevailing order that he jeopardized his life.

From the beginning of the ministry of this itinerant Jewish teacher, Jesus was clearly a person apart not just by his disregard of certain laws and conventions, but by his affirmation of who he was. His words did indeed have the ring of authority as he declared after reading the Jubilee passage in Isaiah 61, "Today in your very hearing this text has come true" (Luke 4:21, NEB).

Jesus was indeed more than the enfleshment of the Jubilee. He was the inbreaking of the future of God because he was the Son of God. In Jesus Christ "the Word became flesh; he came to dwell among us, and we saw his glory, such glory as befits the Father's only Son, full of grace and truth" (John 1:14, NEB).

It was not just Jesus'words that set him apart but his acts as well. He never walked away from human need but always responded with compassion.

Jesus also performed miracles. In our scientific society in which everything is apparently explicable, we struggle with the One who supernaturally healed the sick, set free the possessed, and calmed the sea. Yet we believe Jesus to be God's own Son and, therefore, more than just a teacher. I suspect that's why so many of us take the risk to follow him and learn from him.

Both in substance and methodology the Master Teacher gives those of us who would be disciple makers a compelling model to follow. When he first calls his disciples to follow, he does not suggest an adult education class in discipleship they can attend when they have a free evening. Surprisingly, Jesus' first call is an invitation to radical lifestyle change, to the abandoning of job security, family, and home to join a band of unemployed itinerants. In place of economic security they learned to trust God for their every need, sharing what they received with the poor. In place of a family, they became a family—brothers and sisters bonded together in common cause. In place of a home, the world became their home. Their friends were comprised of those from the fringes of Jewish society. Like Jesus, this first community of followers became a people apart.

Unlike the rabbinic schools that focused on the Torah, Jesus himself became the window on God's truth. He called men and women to follow him. He became the living curriculum in his discipleship school. And he still is the curriculum. Even so, those of us who would be disciple makers must realize that in spite of our brokenness and failure, we are to pray that, through the power of the Spirit, something of Christ's grace will show through in our lives too. What we teach can never be separated from who we are and how we live.

Even as Jesus was the vision of God in his proclamation that the kingdom of God had broken into history with love and power, that must be our vision too. Jesus Christ lived out his life with transparent purpose and commitment. As he discipled his followers, he seemed to have a clear sense of the outcomes God wanted in their lives as a part of that larger kingdom mission that absolutely possessed him.

So his curriculum focused upon God and upon God's kingdom, and his life became a window through which we could glimpse something of God's loving intentions.

As disciple makers, we don't follow a particular theory, we follow a person, a person who fully disclosed God's love and purposes to us. Not surprisingly that changes *us*.

Consistent with the incarnational content of our curriculum, Jesus shares truth more as story than idea. This is not to say that Jesus was anti-intellectual, but he did approach theology more as story, image, and parable than as concept. His whole approach to faith and life immediately impresses us as being more in touch with both faith and life. There's no "ivory tower intellectualizing" in the teaching of this Master, no Hellenistic sophistry, no hair-splitting theological debate. Jesus worked from life itself. He drew his content from the Galilean hillsides and familiar human events.

His amazing parables both disclose and obscure the truth of God. For those who are turning toward God, insight and understanding grows. Jesus helped his disciples to find the meaning in some of the parables he taught, as does the Spirit today. For those not turning toward God, however, the parables have little meaning at all; their gems are hidden.

Even so, Jesus used paradox to communicate with those who would see something of God's design. "It is in losing life that we find life," he taught. Life is achieved through cross-bearing death. That paradoxical assertion makes no more sense to those outside of faith today than when he first spoke it, but for those who have decided to follow, those words contain life itself.

In a very real sense Christ's entire life, death, and resurrection are as disclosing and obscuring as his parables and paradoxes. Those inclined toward God are given to know the "mysteries of the kingdom," but for those "without eyes to see," the cross is indeed "foolishness to those who are perishing." Unlike the rabbinic schools, Jesus' school of discipleship was no more structured or formal than life itself. Similar to what is called nonformal education in developing countries, Jesus' pedagogy was situational. In nonformal education, the instructor waits for a crisis, event, or happening and then uses that situation as a learning opportunity. That's what Jesus did. He used confrontation, crisis, and everyday life situations as learning opportunities.

Obviously, if you plan to have this kind of situational learning process with the people you are discipling, you are going to have to spend a lot of time with them, as Jesus did.

Jesus also taught by giving his disciples responsibility appropriate to their maturity. Too many of our Western learning modes are not only highly structured and intellectual but they are also often "passive/receptive" in style. In other words, the learner in our Christian education systems passively receives someone else's ideas but is not often given an opportunity to participate. If disciples are going to grow, they need to be given real responsibility, particularly in using their gifts in ministry.

Perhaps Jesus taught most compellingly through his own servanthood. As they saw him heal, feed, touch, lift, and, indeed, wash their feet, the disciples saw most transparently what it meant to love and follow God.

As we follow Christ into the challenging responsibility of "making disciples of all nations," we realize how much we have to learn, not only about our own faith but also about how to enable others to follow Jesus Christ in a way that makes a difference for the kingdom in the world both today and tomorrow.

We also realize and need to be reminded that in this, our discipleship and the discipling of others, we are not alone. At the end of his ministry Jesus told his disciples, ". . . it is for your good that I am leaving you. If I do not go, your Advocate will not come, whereas if I go, I will send him to you . . ." (John 16:7-8, NEB).

Just what would happen if we decided to take discipleship seriously? What would happen if we joined those first disciples and enthusiastically put everything else aside to respond to the radical call of Jesus Christ?

What would happen if we joined the thousands of Christians today who are placing Christ and his kingdom at the center of life and not at the periphery; who are inviting Christ to transform not only their spiritual condition but also their cultural values, personal priorities, and the stewardship of their time and resources; who are creating imaginative ways to invest their lives in regular ministry to others and join in small groups where they are known, loved, and supported as they take new risks for the kingdom?

What would happen if our churches joined that growing number of congregations moving beyond institutional maintenance to concentrate on mission and discipleship; who are finding creative ways to make a kingdom difference in their communities and their world?

I will tell you what would happen. Our churches would begin to experience the renewing power of the Spirit of God as we recommit ourselves to the agenda of God. You and others in your church would begin to discover what many others are discovering—that the most satisfying life is the life given away. The Spirit of God would blow through our lives and churches, turning the world upside down again. We would see the hungry fed, the disabled made whole, and the good news proclaimed.

You are invited to join those first disciples and thousands of others in setting aside every lesser thing and seeking first the kingdom of God in response to the escalating challenges of the eighties and nineties. Welcome to the adventure of celebration of the kingdom of God that is changing the world!

Questions for Discussion

1. What was Christ's style of pedagogy as he discipled those first believers?

2. What are the ways we can be disciple-makers today?

3. What, specifically, are you going to do in your life to become more serious about your discipleship and to help others with theirs?

Send your stories of discipleship and ideas for community to: Tom Sine, P.O. Box 9123, Seattle, WA 98109.